Mike Hutton is the author of three novels, *Stripped Assets*, *Dirty Linen* and *The Vice Captain*, published by Book Guild Publishing. In addition to writing he has a life-long interest in early twentieth-century British art, and is part-owner of a National Hunt racehorse. He lives on the borders of Northamptonshire and Leicestershire.

TWENTIES LONDON

Sex, Shopping and Suburban Dreams

Mike Hutton

Book Guild Publishing
Sussex, England

First published in Great Britain in 2011 by
The Book Guild Ltd
Pavilion View
19 New Road
Brighton, BN1 1UF

Typesetting in Garamond by
Keyboard Services, Luton, Bedfordshire

Printed in Spain under the supervision of
MRM Graphics Ltd, Winslow, Bucks

A catalogue record for this book is available from
The British Library

ISBN 978 1 84624 577 0

Contents

Acknowledgements

I should like to thank the following for their invaluable help:

Susan Scott, Archivist, The Savoy Hotel
Gerrie Pitt, Director of Public Relations, The Ritz Hotel
Judy Faraday, Archivist, The John Lewis Partnership
Audrey Snell, Archivist, Wimbledon Lawn Tennis Museum
Patrick Chaplin, Darts Historian
The staff at the Museum of London
The staff at the London Transport Museum
The staff at Westminster City Archives
The Archive Department, Harrods, Knightsbridge
The staff at the Fine Art Society
Bruce Calvert, Silent Film Historian

Also:

My friend Roger Fry for his constant help
Maurice Poole for his generous help and encouragement
Joan Beretta for transcribing my illegible writing and for her expert advice on photographs of the period

Also:

Various members of my family, now sadly no longer with us

Preface

'*When a man is tired of London, he is tired of life.*'
(Samuel Johnson, 1777)

I still cringe in shame at the thought. As an unthinking eleven-year-old I mocked and laughed as my chemistry master fought for breath. His normally pallid complexion turned puce. A class, which had only moments before been imitating the poor man's frantic arm movements as the attack overwhelmed him, fell silent. Frightening yellow mucus flowed from his nose. Bent double, it gushed from his mouth, spattering onto the exercise books piled on his desk. I ran forward with another lad, realising something was dreadfully wrong. As we went to help him he fought us off with an almost demented strength. Wide-eyed and shaking, he roared, 'You little bastards, have you never heard of mustard gas?' He staggered to the door. We never saw him again.

That incident etched so firmly in my mind, took place in 1949, thirty years after the end of the Great War. Scarcely a British family emerged unscathed from the carnage. My father's eldest brother, who had left his home in Marylebone with such confidence, was dead within six months of reaching France. Killed in action, the telegram had said, and my grandmother went to her grave some fifty years later still believing him to be a hero. He may well have been, and he was killed in action, but not the sort she would have been proud of, as she was an avid member of the Temperance Society.

It appears that uncle Fred was given a forty-eight hour pass away from the trenches. Unfortunately, he and a few mates missed their transport back to the front line, so they 'borrowed' a horse and cart.

It was not until roll-call the following morning that Fred was missed. He was found later having died of exposure in a ditch. He had witnessed rather more exposure earlier that evening as he had been a customer of the local brothel. Luckily, my grandmother was never told. These, and other stories like them, would have been commonplace, although many returning home never spoke of what they had endured. It was time to move on. Although it was reported that in many parts of the country the end of hostilities was greeted with sober self-restraint, London was different. Here champagne was quaffed in the West End, whilst further east the brewers struggled to keep up with demand.

A year later, as the new decade dawned, London was, as ever, a complex mass of contradictions. A conglomeration of distinct villages forged together as a seething whole. Noisy, impatient. On the surface, grand, but underneath often mean and violent. At once stylish, industrious, quick-witted, yet outrageous, immoral and cruel. Londoners, from whatever background, were determined to put the war years behind them and have a good time.

Welcome to the 1920s. It's going to be an exciting ride...

1

Introducing The Cast

'Flowers are as common in the country,
As people are in London.'

(Oscar Wilde)

It's Thursday. Not a sign of any blue sky. A rather cold, drab Thursday.
Staff at London's grandest hotels are still clearing the debris from the
night's celebrations. Although it's almost seven o'clock, the last of the
revellers have only just staggered off to bed. Barbara Cartland may
have described the Ritz as 'rather stuffy', but the dining-room is still
festooned with fallen streamers and burst balloons. This is a special
Thursday, no matter how drab. The first, not only of a new year,
but of a new decade.

About a mile away, a sixteen-year-old girl is being woken by the
rattle of metal wheels on the road outside her window. That young
girl is my mother, the year 1920. The noise on the street is caused
by the barrow boys racing down Church Street to get the best pitch
for the day. The older traders employ fit, strong youngsters who
shout, swear and laugh as they career down the road. From downstairs
comes the comforting smell of baking bread. Her father (my grandfather)
has been up since five o'clock overseeing batches of steam loaves
together with trays of pumpernickel and rye bread. After breakfast
she will serve in the shop until lunchtime, but then she has the
afternoon off. At two o'clock, she sets off towards Edgware Road.
Church Street is full of stalls selling a huge range of essential and
exotic goods. Fruit and vegetables predominate, but there is popular
sheet music for sale, lengths of dress fabric, a stall selling wool and
reels of cotton. Butchers with blood-stained aprons stand sharpening

Doris Russell, the baker's daughter from Church Street.

An Italian ice-cream seller and friend.

their knives. She hears the chatter of caged birds; canaries and a grey parrot are for sale. The street is busy now; housewives prod, feel and smell the produce. Cockney voices shout out their offers, ''Ere you are, lady, two pound of sugar, one and six, no, I tell you what, how about one and three?' The dentist has set up his stall, which proclaims extractions at 1/- or 2/- for painless, the only difference being the roll of a drum to deaden the cries of the patient.

She turns left into Edgware Road and hurries towards Marble Arch. Everyone seems to be rushing. A sea of cloth caps, the occasional bowler, then the glimpse of a Homburg pulled down over a solemn face, a couple of trilbys worn at a rakish angle. Gentlemen with twirled umbrellas push past housewives window-shopping. Unshaven men, pasty faced with 'roll your own' fags fixed firmly in their mouths. Everyone seems to project the background they come from or, perhaps, just aspire to. Huge red buses, some open topped, roar and growl, picking their way through the clanging trams. Motor cars splutter and fight for space, whilst the drivers of the horse-drawn cabs tug at the reins in the hope of their scrawny horses finding some open road. There are shoeshine boys, and gypsies selling violets from wicker baskets.

Turning into Oxford Street, the shops become smarter. Massive stores rising like palaces, their windows crammed again after the shortages of the war years. Crowds of people clog the pavements. Young women with figures like boys. Nannies in uniform pushing unwieldy black prams. An organ grinder with a monkey on a chain. A band of ex-servicemen, medals on their chests, walking in the gutter, cars rushing by only inches from running them down. This is live theatre with an ever-changing cast of thousands. Who are these people that my mother described to me? Are they so different from the Londoners of today? It was a world where it was still possible to identify people by their dress. The Great War had been a catalyst for change. Vast swathes of British youth from all social backgrounds were lost. Death did not discriminate by class; junior officers were the most vulnerable in battle and thousands of potential leaders were killed.

The working-class Londoners

It's the cockney that most of us think of when describing a true Londoner. Depending on who you believe, Old English 'cockeney' referred to an effeminate man, or, as most Londoners would prefer, a 'townee'. Our 1920s version is generally short in stature and sharp of mind. He has been described as smart, flash and streetwise. Also as rebellious, irreverent, brazen and bolshie. By 1933 H. J. Massingham quoted in *The London Scene* notes, 'His astuteness, nonchalance, easy insufficient fellowship, bonhomie, casual endurance, grumbling gusto, shallowness, unconcern for anything but the passing moment, jackdaw love of glitter, picaresque adaptability and jesting spirit make up a unique individual.' His female counterpart is just as sharp, both in appearance and wit. 'She tries to get her hands on any money he makes before he drinks it "down the boozer".' Mind you, she won't say no to an odd glass of stout or a couple of port and lemons herself. Although slum clearance is underway, many of the ancient rookeries still exist and thousands of London's poor live in close proximity to their posh neighbours. Filthy, narrow alleys and crowded courtyards, where the sun never penetrates and sanitation is confined to an outside tap, still lurk in the shadows. The smells are those of medieval England rather than a twentieth-century city.

Middle-class aspirations

The emerging middle class man, who gains ground rapidly throughout the 1920s, tends to be pictured as a Pooterish type of character, with well-formed social aspirations. Typically, he is a clerk or a rather successful artisan. He is the guardian of outward respectability who, increasingly during the decade, migrates to the suburbs and 'Metroland'. He wears stiff white collars and a shiny suit, with a newer one in the wardrobe reserved for Sundays and funerals. He longs for a semi in Putney or Hendon, and dreams one day of owning his own motor car. His wife or girlfriend is a changed woman, thanks to the war. Many women took men's jobs during the hostilities. They have subsequently become quite liberated in their own minds, with a vote by the time they are thirty (it was 1928 before women gained the same voting rights as men). They dismiss outright the thought of going back into service. This group of women are far too smart for that, they are taking up jobs as shop assistants or working in offices. They learn shorthand and typing, and become fashion conscious and go to the cinema. Whilst the feckless working class and the degenerate nobs indulge in all sorts of beastly activity, it is left to this group to safeguard the moral standing of the country. Well, that's what those of us who were brought up by them were led to believe. Maybe they protested too much!

All too much for the toffs

Snobbery was rampant in the 1920s and the aristocracy, squirearchy and 'old money' really objected to those who had made fortunes during the war. They sneered at their accents, their dress and their frightful table manners. They resented these self-made men who had prospered whilst their sons and friends had suffered at the front. They were horrified as this small, but influential, group started buying up some of London's finest houses and country estates, many of which had been in the same families for centuries. Much of this activity had been brought on by the threat of increased death duties. They talked about these *nouveau riche* behind their backs. They scoffed and sometimes belittled them but, dammit, they couldn't be ignored. This was a new breed of men – hard, industrious and single minded, just the qualities that many representing the 'old money' singularly lacked. Maybe the threat of these foul death duties, coupled with the fact that the pound was only worth 8/6 in comparison to the days before the war, had led to some establishment figures selling up or downsizing, but the dukes, viscounts, barons, lords and ladies were not about to be sidelined so easily. They sought expert advice and retrenched.

It was their young who led the way in putting the ghastly war behind them. They were out to have a good time. These youngsters felt truly liberated and their parents, understandably, looked on in horror as they set about breaking all the social rules ever invented.

They attacked life with a reckless disregard for propriety or their own health. They consumed vast quantities of champagne and cocktails. Drugs were used to keep the party spirit alive. They discovered sex and decided they liked it. Although it was 1934 before Cole Porter wrote the lyrics for 'Anything Goes', it perfectly captured the mood of this crazy, post-war generation, who were hell bent on enjoying themselves.

An old friend of mine from a well-to-do family, who was a young woman in London in the 1920s, insisted the talk of today's permissive society was nonsense. Before she died she informed me, with a naughty glint in her eye, 'Believe me, they can't invent anything today that we didn't try.' 'I do mean anything,' she repeated, with emphasis. Looking up at a portrait of her as an eighteen-year-old, all blonde hair, buttoned lip and an air of innocence, I found it hard to believe. She caught my eye. 'That was for my parents. Chocolate-box, don't you think? Sorry, Mike, I was a vamp. Do you want more tea?'

The outsiders

So to the final characters in our London cast – the immigrants. Somehow the British still perpetuate the myth that we welcome foreigners into our midst. Throughout our history this has never been so, but we are maybe marginally more tolerant than other countries. Being such a major port has probably influenced the number of foreigners who have settled in London. If we go back far enough in our family histories, it is unlikely that many of us are purely English, Scottish or Welsh. My own family has a trinity of Irish, German and French to add to our English roots.

In the East End it was the Jews that formed the largest and most influential community. Some of the worst slums in London were still to be found in Whitechapel, Stratford and Bethnal Green. Many Jewish families worked in crowded sweatshops producing fine clothes for their wealthy West End neighbours. Yiddish was widely spoken because they had come from many different countries right across Europe. The Portuguese and Spanish Jews were amongst the first to arrive, to be followed by those escaping pogroms and persecution in Germany, Holland, Poland, Russia and the rest of Eastern Europe. There was a particularly large population of Russians and Poles in Stepney. Lew and Bernard Winogradsky were raised in Brick Lane and ended up Baron Grade and Baron Delfont of Bethnal Green. Rich and famous they became, but they never forgot their humble roots. The East End was also home to a sizeable Chinese community. In the 1920s, Limehouse, situated right by the docks, was known as Chinatown. Today, partly because of war damage and also the redevelopment of the docklands, Chinatown has migrated to the area around Gerrard Street in Soho. The housing in Limehouse was dreadful even by East End standards and many Londoners were dubious about visiting the area, with endless tales of extreme violence and opium taking.

It's natural for immigrants to form their own communities in what is often, initially, a hostile environment. The potato famine in the 1840s saw huge numbers of Irish leave the Emerald Isle. Those arriving in London congregated largely around Kilburn and the poorer areas of Paddington and Marylebone. These districts were dominated by their own pubs, clubs and cultural activities. The Irish also found their way to St Giles and Soho, London's most cosmopolitan area. This exotic Square Mile in London's West End attracted foreigners escaping victimisation as well as the artistic; the louche, drunkards and criminals. The Greeks were the first to arrive in the 1680s to escape the religious persecution of the Ottoman Turks. Greek Street still survives today, despite being described in 1906 as one of the very worst streets in London. A royal commission stated that 'crowds gather there nightly who are little else than a pest.' It concluded that 'some of the vilest reptiles in London live there and frequent it.'

By 1920 little appears to have changed. Whilst there were doubtless many honest, hard-working Italians living in Soho, it was gangs run by their countrymen who controlled many of the rackets in the West End. There was also a sizeable Italian colony living on what had been, in centuries past, the marshy land of Clerkenwell. Initially, on arrival, they tended to work in the tiling or mosaic trades, whilst others were organ or knife grinders. Gradually, they moved into catering, selling food on the streets and opening restaurants as they prospered. They were renowned for their superb ice cream, which was by far the best in London. The largest community in Soho was the French. Descendants of the Huguenots, they had become successful not only in the wine and restaurant trades, but also as craftsmen in wood carving and as gunsmiths. Elsewhere in London, there were pockets of white Russians and Scandinavians. Rich Americans also headed for London as part of their European tour. So this toxic mix of players was ready to seek compensation for the ghastly years that had just passed. It was time to have some fun.

Brenda Dean Paul.

2

Party Time

'The moon belongs to everyone,
The best things in life are free,
The stars belong to everyone,
They gleam there for you and me.

The flowers in the spring,
The robins that sing,
The sunbeam that shines,
They're yours, they're mine.'

(Song by B. G. DeSilva, Len Brown and Ray Henderson, 1927)

The bright young people of the 1920s didn't believe a word of these popular lyrics. It was 1924 when the *Daily Mail* coined the phrase 'Bright Young People' who, in turn, became more commonly known as 'Bright Young Things'. Somehow, this small group came to represent the spirit of 'The Roaring Twenties'. It also seems pretty certain that if we had been around at the time most of us would have wholeheartedly loathed them. Initially, this loosely defined group was drawn from extremely rich and well-connected families. By the end of the decade they had been joined by a more raffish, bohemian set and an army of hangers-on. It was statutory for the young women to affect a look of extreme boredom as they stared out from under their cloche hats. As the day progressed and the cocktails began to flow they tended to become more animated, noisy and opinionated, or just plain vacuous. Barbara Cartland defended them, saying, 'Quite frankly, I think that the "Bright Young People" brought a great deal of brightness into a world which was sadly in need of it.'

The men on the whole seemed a strange lot. They appeared feckless, foppish and vapid, with more than a hint of homosexuality thrown in for good measure. They spoke in a meticulously enunciated drawl. Much of their outlandish behaviour was blamed on the war, whose shadow still hung heavily over the country. Perhaps their antics were an overreaction, an attempt to relegate the devastation that had been visited on almost every family in the country, no matter how grand. The origin of the group dates back to the early twenties. It revolved around a small, rich, exclusive clan including the beautiful, disdainful and wayward Elizabeth Ponsonby and her cousin Loelia, the Jungman sisters, Lady Eleanor Smith and a selection of Guinnesses.

Elizabeth Ponsonby and the Bright Young Things

Evelyn Waugh comments on meeting Elizabeth Ponsonby for the first time in October 1925. He notes rather archly that 'Two years ago I should have been rather thrilled by her.' He continues, 'We drank red wine which made us unwell.' By January of the following year he records, 'Rather to my surprise, but considerably to my gratification, Elizabeth Ponsonby made vigorous love to me which I am sorry now I did not accept.' 'She has furry arms,' he added, not telling us if this was an attraction, or a turn-off.

Elizabeth's family were distinguished, well born but relatively poor by upper-class standards. Her mother's father was the composer Sir Hubert Parry, whilst her grandfather on her father's side had been private secretary to Queen Victoria. Her own father was a distinguished politician who, later in his career, was to become Labour leader of the House of Lords. No matter, she was destined to drive them to despair by her louche behaviour as was Eleanor Smith the daughter of Lord Birkenhead, and the Jungman girls who were connected to the Guinness family through their mother's second marriage.

Of the men who were prominent in the group from the very beginning, perhaps Brian Howard is one of the most interesting. Born in Surrey of wealthy American parents, he travelled the traditional route of Eton and Oxford, only to arrive on the London scene with a wide circle of influential friends, including Lord David Cecil and Harold Acton. An aspiring poet, he was amusing, outrageous and

The disdainful and wayward Elizabeth Ponsonby, who was a leading light of 'The Bright Young People'. Her father was a senior figure in the Labour government.

effete. A social butterfly who, at the thought of having to work, informed his mother he would kill himself rather than become a journalist. Strangely, later in life he became a regular contributor to the *New Statesman*.

As usual, it was the *Daily Mail* who latched onto one of the group's early escapades, no doubt sensing that this collection of privileged youngsters would continue to be newsworthy. The event involved a rather elaborate treasure hunt. The 'Bright Young People' appeared to think it hilarious, chasing all over London looking for clues on public transport that few of them had ever used before. Double-decker buses and the Underground were exciting new territory. Nothing like a little slumming now and again! Later, these hunts became ever more elaborate involving up to fifty cars charging around the streets of London at break-neck speed. Whilst annoying, these jaunts were put down to youthful exuberance, although the press interest raised some concern. It was the escalating themed parties, however, that changed perceptions. Their parents looked on in alarm as the young jettisoned all their social manners in a frantic whirl of unthinking enjoyment.

For the most part, the country remained staunchly Conservative in outlook. Youngsters, even those from privileged backgrounds, were expected to conform as previous generations had done (at least on the surface). This sudden explosion of having fun at any cost, and often to the irritation of others, was foreign to most. It seemed, at the very least, unthinking after the massive loss of life and hideous injuries sustained during the war. When Gertrude Stein referred to the 'lost generation', she was aiming her fire at contemporary writers, but it could just as well have been directed at this dissolute group of young people in London. In a sense they were truly lost, often in a blur of cocktails and champagne. The parties became increasingly contentious. There was a real scandal covered by the press where a mixed bathing party was conducted whilst being watched by a negro band. There were stupid scavenging parties culminating in a challenge to bring back a pipe belonging to prime minister Stanley Baldwin. Mission completed! It was the advent of the bottle party, but guests were also expected to bring rather more exotic fare, perhaps caviar or a few dozen oysters. There were Victorian parties, Wild West

Some 'Bright Young Things' attending a themed baby party.

parties and, more shockingly, Roman orgy parties. Baby parties became popular, with guests arriving in nappies. The most extravagant party recorded was given by the young Norman Hartnell. His theme was the circus. Hartnell came from a relatively modest background. His parents were publicans. A creative youngster, he had already started his fashion house by 1923. Perhaps because of this, like his upwardly mobile friend Cecil Beaton, he was welcomed into the expanding group of 'Bright Young Things'. A unique talent as well as money was capable of opening doors.

For his party, he hired a house in Bruton Street. The diaries of Evelyn Waugh record: 'The guests discovered that the premises had been decorated in the style of a fairground. The booths displayed live animals including a dancing bear, a seal and a Siberian wolf. There was dancing to a circus orchestra, a jazz band and an Italian accordion quartet, while the guests included Lady Dean Paul and her daughter Brenda dressed by designer Willy Clarkson as, respectively, a Lyons waitress and a female wrestler.' The whole event must have cost a fortune. Norman was obviously already charging healthy prices for his frocks!

Let's face the music and dance

Doubtless, the guests danced the Charleston, which had arrived from the States four years previously in 1925, although originally dismissed in London as frightfully vulgar. The *Dancing Times* organised a special tea dance at the Carnival Club in Dean Street. Here, some sixty teachers were employed to try to spread the news of this wild, new dance. Gradually, it became more popular, although most found its steps difficult to negotiate. It was the Prince of Wales – a talented dancer – who catapulted the Charleston into a craze. Everyone under thirty felt under pressure to conquer it. Hours were spent in countless homes performing the steps. Within a few months the Charleston was *de rigueur* at every social gathering where there was music. It was visiting black musicians from the States who set the benchmark for natural ability and they were watched with a mixture of fascination and envy by the generally uncoordinated upper crust. The dance was open to interpretation. For a few opening choruses you held your partner, but then you drifted apart and added steps of your own invention. The frantic exercise helped make a few 'lounge lizards' fitter as they cavorted around the floor. A leading cleric declared that anyone who loved beauty would rather die than be associated with the Charleston. Dancing had become a national obsession: ballroom, tap, Charleston or shimmy.

> *'If I could shimmy like my sister Kate,*
> *Shake it like a jelly on a plate,*
> *My mamma wanted to know last night,*
> *How sister Kate could do it so nice.*
> *Now all the boys in the neighbourhood*
> *Knew Kate could shimmy, and it's mighty good,*
> *I may be late but I'll be up to date,*
> *When I can shimmy like my sister Kate,*
> *I mean shake it like my sister Kate.'*

('I Wish I Could Shimmy Like My Sister Kate' – words by Clarence Williams and Armand Piron; popularised by Anna Jones and Fats Waller)

So, wherever you went in the twenties, there was always somewhere to dance, either at an elegant tea dance or a rather shady Palais de Danse. Another craze was created by the Black Bottom. This was a foot stomping dance from America's deep south. The foxtrot remained popular, as did the one-step and, of course, the ultimate in dramatic dancing, the tango. This was largely due to the incredible popularity of Rudolph Valentino who danced like a god, but treated his women with disdain. An irresistible combination, apparently. The poshest tea dances in London were held at the Café de Paris or the Savoy, which both charged a hefty 5/-, whilst the rather downmarket Regent Palace would only set you back 2/-, but the clientele were thought to be a bit iffy. No 'Bright Young Thing' would be seen dead there.

It's not all black and white, you know...

Although there was a very real colour prejudice in Britain, black performers were increasingly given access to the 'Bright Young People'. Society remained sharply class conscious and xenophobic. Few Britons had ever come into contact with 'natives', as coloured people were usually described. The very colour black carried with it warnings. Black moods, black holes, darkness, danger. There were whispered tales of their primitive sexual prowess. It sent a collective shiver through the young ladies but, as we shall see, some of those shivers were in anticipation rather than fear. A painting by the Scottish artist John Souter caused outrage at the summer exhibition of the Royal Academy in 1926. His painting *The Breakdown* depicted a black musician sitting astride a prone statue of the goddess Minerva. That was surely bad enough, but he was staring at a white girl dancing the Charleston *stark naked*! The painting was removed on the instructions of the Colonial Office, no less. Shortly after this upset, Paul and Essie Robeson were asked to leave the Savoy Grill as other diners had objected. He was fine, in their eyes, singing 'Ole Man River', but that was as far as they would or could keep their prejudices in check.

Evelyn Waugh seems to have had a different view; he is quoted as saying that 'a party without a black wasn't a party'. An entry in his diary for February 1927 records him going to see *Blackbirds*, a hit show with a troupe of black performers led by Florence Mills. In terms unacceptable today, he recalls 'other niggers and negresses' being in the dressing-room. Then onto a night-club called Victor's, to see another 'nigger Leslie Hutchinson' (Hutch).

The British Empire Exhibition was opened on St George's Day 1924 by King George V. It was promoted as a serious attempt to stimulate trade. To the 'Bright Young People' trade was something of a dirty word. Not for them a trawl around the palace of industry. Rather, a boisterous group of them made for the adjoining funfair. They hired boats to go through the river caves, which was like an upmarket tunnel of love with decoration based on Dante's *Inferno*. They overturned their boats and paddled around, to other visitors' annoyance, bizarrely playing ukuleles. Later, the same group, no doubt still bedraggled, made their way to their more familiar territory of the West End. Here, they enjoyed themselves playing 'Follow my Leader' through Selfridges. They climbed all over the counters, sending displays crashing to the floor. Middle England looked on muttering at the juvenile stupidity of these spoilt youngsters. Although the incident was widely reported, Gordon Selfridge didn't complain. To him there was no such thing as bad publicity.

The public were less forgiving. Although Norman Hartnell's party had been offensively lavish, it was an event earlier that year that tipped the balance. A mock wedding was the brainchild of Elizabeth Ponsonby. The party was held at the Trocadero on Shaftesbury Avenue. The themed dress seemed innocuous enough. Guests were invited to turn up in clothes in vogue eight years previously in 1921. Elizabeth was to play 'the bride', whilst the 'best man', Robert Byron, arrived sporting a caddish waxed moustache and wearing a brown bowler hat. John Rayner acted as the 'groom' and Oliver Messel and an assortment of socialites represented the noisy congregation. Tellingly, an unsuspecting clergyman was pulled off the street to perform the blessing.

To modern sensibilities, this charade seems merely crass and juvenile, but lurid newspaper coverage prompted public outrage. Middle England was horrified. Whilst many people had battled through the worst of the depression and were still experiencing hardship, these supposed 'Bright Young People' appeared oblivious to anything but their own self-centred world. This was decadent, offensive behaviour by a group of rich, spoilt youngsters. The parents of those involved ducked for cover. This single event crystallised what they had been telling their offspring for years. They had sunk into a meaningless, self-absorbed, degenerate existence. This spoilt group of young people, which probably numbered little more than a thousand in all, had turned its back on everything its parents' generation valued. They spent their lives dancing, going to crazy parties, consorting with blacks and the dross of society. They trashed houses, stubbed cigarettes out on antique furniture and peed on the flowerbeds. They had the morals of alley cats and had no purpose to their lives.

Evelyn Waugh states in his diary: 'The test of a young man's worth is the insolence he could carry off without mishap.' In September 1926 he records: 'In the evening we went to the Alhambra and then onto a party given by the lesbian girls I met the other day. Sir Francis Larking, dressed first as a girl and then stark naked, attempted the Charleston.' Towards the end of the twenties, gatecrashers were making inroads and sometimes parties ended in marauding, running fights. It couldn't go on. But it did for a time, anyway.

Sex, drugs and Long Island Ice Tea

Sex has always been with us and some think it was the twenties' generation that pointed the way towards the permissive society. Although we know the 'Bright Young People' sometimes attended orgy parties, there is little evidence that this is how the average evening ended. Doubtless, servicemen home on short leave from the front during the war had led to a change in the moral compass. It was reckoned that up to ten per cent of young people carried contraceptives in vanity cases or wallets. Homosexuality, although illegal, appears to have been quite common amongst the smart set. Brian Howard, the occasional poet and dauber, was described as *'mad, bad and dangerous'* by Evelyn Waugh. He was certainly outwardly extremely camp, as were many of the group. Oliver Messel, Norman Hartnell, Cecil Beaton – the list goes on.

Doctor Marie Stopes was attempting to popularise birth control. But her critics were horrified. A book by W. N. Willis, *Wedded Love or Married Misery* trumpeted the need for every ounce of British flesh and bone to replenish the depleted stock so savaged by the Great War. So no wasted effort, no hanky panky! Fine, new children were needed to take the place of the fallen in running the Empire. No thanks, chorused the 'Bright Young People'.

A new delight from the States stemmed the growth in sales of champagne for a time. Enter the cocktail. Before the war a dry sherry was just about acceptable before supper. Perhaps it was the dreary standard of cooking served in most British homes that led to the cocktail's runaway success. A symbol of the twenties is the white-jacketed barman pouring a Sidecar or Manhattan. The French chef André Simon declared that one cocktail helps the appetite, but two or three harms the flow of gastric juices. The 'Bright Young Things' took to cocktails like ducks to water. Why stop at three?

Drugs also played their part and this certainly didn't help counter the growing perception that the smart set in London's social hierarchy had gone too far. Drugs had always been a part of the London scene.

Brilliant Chang, notorious drug dealer, restaurateur and womaniser.

Laudanum and opium were freely available during the nineteenth century. Conan Doyle's famous detective Sherlock Holmes was described as regularly injecting himself, with scarcely an eyebrow raised. Yet London in the twenties was gripped by a general panic about heroin and cocaine abuse. A hearty distrust of foreigners pointed the finger at the Chinese community. They had tended to settle in Limehouse, and there was much talk of squalid opium dens, with decent English girls being spirited away to a fate worse than death in some filthy, foreign brothel. Beware the Yellow Peril!

It was a Chinese man known as Brilliant Chang who became the centre of attention in 1922. A young dance teacher, Freda Kempton, was found dead from an overdose of cocaine. It was proved that Chang had been with her the night before. He told the coroner, 'She was a friend of mine. I know nothing of cocaine. It's all a mystery to me.' The coroner decided that there was not enough evidence to convict Chang but added 'that it was disgraceful that such a dangerous drug as cocaine should be bandied around London to ruin the bodies and souls of inexperienced girls'. Chang was a good-looking charmer, but he had form. He had been connected to the death of the actress Billie Carleton after she had attended a victory ball at the Albert Hall in November 1918. The drug had been given to her by her boyfriend Reggie de Vieuille. His suppliers were a Chinese man called Lau Ping Yu and his Scottish wife Ada, who were known associates of Chang. The Marlborough Street magistrate obviously decided Ada was largely responsible, sentencing her to five months' hard labour, while her husband was only fined £10. He also described Ada as 'the High Priestess of unholy rites'. De Vieuille admittted to conspiracy to supply cocaine and was sentenced to eight years' hard labour at the Old Bailey.

It was the *World Pictorial News* that drew the public's attention to Chang, describing how 'he dispensed Chinese delicacies and the drugs and vices of the Orient at his fashionable restaurant in Regent Street' (now part of the Austin Reed store).

Chang also had a restaurant in Gerrard Street opposite Mrs Kate Meyrick's notorious 43 Club, where it was rumoured that members were able to freely purchase their drug of choice. The adverse publicity, including calls for the deportation of all Chinese, forced Chang to retreat to the Chinese stronghold of Limehouse. There he opened the Shanghai restaurant and he continued to form a network dispensing drugs all over London. In 1924, his premises were raided by the police and large quantities of cocaine were discovered. Chang was jailed for eighteen months and, on his release, deported. It was reckoned that he continued to control the London drug scene from Paris. It was estimated that he pocketed in excess of a staggering £1 million. He was arrested again in Paris in 1927 for drug dealing. True to form, he skipped bail and disappeared along with a pretty young woman and was never heard of again.

It is not clear how widespread the use of drugs was among the burgeoning numbers who, by the end of the decade, referred to themselves as 'Bright Young People'. We have to assume that some of Chang's wealth can be ascribed to them. We do know that Hutch, who regularly entertained them, was supposed to have taken heroin, according to fellow pianist Billy Minton. What is certain is that the original 'it girl' Brenda Dean Paul did. Her dependency started on a trip to Paris and thereafter her life careered increasingly out of control until her squalid death in 1959. 'Anything Goes' could have been written for her. She was one of the original 'Bright Young Things', the daughter of a baronet on her mother's side and the granddaughter of a famous Polish violinist. She was introduced to London society in her early teens, including members of the influential Guinness family. Whilst not a conventional beauty, she had a rather cheeky, attractive face and a superb lithe figure. She was outward going and fun, taking on any challenge, no matter how crazy. She also acquired a gift of choosing the wrong men for lovers. She partied non-stop. She rose late for lunchtime cocktails, which merged into champagne swigging at night. When life seemed dull a little white powder helped restore her spirits. She was the ultimate party girl. Sadly, she was probably mentally unbalanced as she set sail on a self-destructive mission for the next high. Hutch was just one of her countless lovers. Whilst at a party in Belgravia in 1927, Hutch hit on the idea of auctioning himself. No prizes for guessing who won. Brenda Dean Paul grabbed him and, to applause, ran up the stairs bursting into the first bedroom they came upon. Their host's parents were not amused as they stared out from under the bedclothes, but Brenda was, Hutch was and so were all the partygoers downstairs. Who cared what the old thought? It was the 'Bright Young People' who counted now. Or was it?

3

Bed and Breakfast

'Children of The Ritz,
Sleek and civilized,
Frightfully surprised;
We know just how we want our quails done
And then we go and have our nails done.'

(Noel Coward – from the review, *Words and Music,* 1932)

The Ritz was not the place for a young girl to go in the evening. There was no band to speak of – not that they could dance to anyway. The social life of the young and fashionable had been transformed. The grand opulence so cherished by the Edwardians was considered 'old hat'. However, an *afternoon* at the hotel was a different proposition. Tea could be fun. According to Barbara Cartland, the cakes were better at Gunters, but the Ritz offered advantages. Perched on high chairs in the Palm Court overlooking the vestibule, the young ladies could spot those entering instantly. It gave them access to those she referred to as 'the also ran men'. Possibly very attractive in themselves, but not from influential backgrounds. Some probably even struggling to raise the 2/6 for the set tea. A hefty price when a jolly good dinner at the Trocadero would only set you back 7/6; and, if venturing into Soho, dinner could be had for as little as 5/-. So, the Ritz was 'stuffy', the Carlton ('heaven help us!') was for businessmen, the Savoy (intriguingly), was 'fast', and several other establishments were 'frankly outrageous'. It was to the Berkeley that the young flocked to dance the night away.

Visitors to London prior to the advent of the railways had tended to stay in lodging houses or rented accommodation. The late nineteenth

Cabaret time at the Savoy for an all-male audience.

The dramatic foyer to The Savoy in 1924.

century witnessed the building of many grand hotels to cater for the increasing numbers of visitors from the shires and abroad. By the beginning of the twenties, many of London's grandest houses had been sold off for redevelopment and these 'old money' families joined the influx of those who needed somewhere to rest their heads when in town. Like many of us, they didn't care much for change and the grand hotels had to deal with complaints about the harshness of electric lighting. Candles were still requested for bedside reading. Some disliked fitted washbasins – how unhygienic to have a basin in the bedroom! When I need water I will call for it, was the cry. But there was no turning back, and though the suites still featured coal fires, tiled bathrooms and showers were fitted throughout.

By the early twenties, the lack of a dance band was causing real concern to the management at the Ritz. Their well-heeled guests were taking a short walk up Bond Street to visit the new Embassy night-club, which had the star attraction of Ambrose and his Band, who would arrive late in the evening, after fulfilling earlier engagements. The owners of the Embassy, sensing an opportunity, contacted the Ritz with a view to leasing the lower ground floor. There was a heated boardroom row. The traditionalists felt the tone of the hotel would be lowered, but there was already considerable unrest about the quality of service the hotel was offering. A compromise was reached with an unexciting string orchestra being introduced in the Palm Court. Hermione Baddeley was not impressed. 'Can't you play something hot?' she implored. Staid the hotel might have been, but the Ritz was a great place for gossip. Michael Arlen had a shave and massage each morning in the hotel's hairdressing salon, and it was here that he gathered much of the background information for his sensational novel, *The Green Hat*. An Armenian by birth, his real name was Dikran Kouyoumdjian. Lady Cunard rather rudely introduced him to a group of friends eating in the restaurant at the hotel as 'the only Armenian who has not been massacred'. Barbara Cartland recalled being shocked by Edwina Mountbatten turning up at the hotel wearing nylon stockings. Then, in 1922, Beverley Nichols noted the Trix sisters wearing beige stockings and overheard some old dowagers commenting that the country had taken another step towards the pit.

The previous year, Charlie Chaplin had made a triumphant return to London after a nine-year absence. He stayed in the first floor Regal Suite and he stood on the balcony throwing carnations down to the huge crowds gathered below. The boy from Walworth had certainly arrived, but this outward worship of celebrity rather offended the Ritz management and, for a time, they didn't encourage showbiz personalities or film stars to stay. Douglas Fairbanks and his son must have passed muster, however, as they continued to be guests at the hotel during the twenties. Literary figures were obviously more welcome and Evelyn Waugh was a regular visitor. It was over dinner in 1927 that he proposed to his first wife. Failing to get into romantic overdrive, he suggested they should get married 'and see how it goes'. It didn't, and they divorced in 1930.

And the band played on...

The Ritz and the Savoy were undoubtedly the most famous London hotels of the era. It was, therefore, somewhat ironic that the Ritz was without a popular in-house band, particularly as it was César Ritz who had first introduced bands and dancing to the Savoy. Ritz had worked for ten years at the Savoy before setting off to open his eponymous hotels in Paris and, subsequently, in Piccadilly. By 1920, dancing was central to a hotel's success and when the Ritz's clients were not hot-footing it to the Embassy, they only had to cross the road to enjoy the entertainment at the Berkeley, which, incidentally, was owned by the Savoy Group.

The Savoy had become synonymous with dance bands. However, the Savoy Quartet, who were in residence in 1920, hardly represented what the new generation of dancers demanded, although they did record 'Swanee' in June of that year. William de Mornys was asked by the management to recruit bands for the hotel to meet the modern demand. Band members often played for different outfits, sometimes even on the same day, to maximise their earnings. Cuban music had become very popular in America and in 1921 Bert Railton arrived in England. A saxophonist, he formed the New York Havana Band and, following appearances at the London Coliseum, was recruited to form the Savoy Havana Band. They were very popular, making numerous recordings,

Les Thés Dansants au Savoy

Tea dances were all the rage and would set you back 5/- in 1927.

The Savoy Havana Band with Cyril Ramon Newton, 1923.

starting with the 'Yankee Doodle Blues' in November 1922. Earlier, in April of that year, they broadcast from a British Broadcasting Company studio for the first time.

It was in 1923 that the Dublin-born pianist and vocalist Debroy Somers was recruited to form his famous Savoy Orpheans Orchestra. Across the country, people tuned into regular weekly broadcasts from the hotel. These not only offered the novelty of live music but the authenticity was heightened by the clapping between dances and the clink of glasses. Rudy Vallee was still paying with the band, as was Cyril Ramon Newton. The Savoy Orpheans reached unprecedented popularity through their broadcasts and made dozens of recordings. Debroy Somers fell foul of the hotel's management in 1926, by touring during the quiet hotel season in January, and insisting on calling his band the Savoy Orpheans, which the hotel claimed as their own. He left the Savoy in April and went on to make numerous recordings with his own band over the years. Cyril Ramon Newton now became leader of the band, but an increasing influence was Carroll Gibbons on piano. Gibbons was an American who came to London to study music. He joined the Orpheans in 1925 and stayed at the Savoy throughout the thirties. He also recorded with the New Mayfair Orchestra for HMV. Many American musicians were now playing in British bands, some undoubtedly to escape prohibition. During the late twenties, Fred Elizalde, a Filipino pianist and band leader, was recruited to lead the Savoy hotel band. He had come, like Gibbons, to study, in his case law at Cambridge University, but, not for the first time, a career in music proved irresistible. He and his band recorded 'An Evening at the Savoy' in 1927.

Listening to many of the old recordings of the various bands who played at the Savoy during the twenties helps recreate the atmosphere of those heady times. Somehow, though, they sound just a little too hearty and, consequently, rather contrived. However, they formed the basis for the really golden era of British dance band music. Ray Noble and the wonderful Al Bowlly were waiting in the wings.

As well as dance bands, the Savoy conjures up images of luxurious bedroom suites, the sophisticated Grill Room and the wonderful views across the Thames. Picture the American Bar. The rattle of ice as the latest cocktail is produced with a theatrical flourish. The hum of conversation, the vague whiff of expensive perfume, somewhat overwhelmed by cigarette smoke. Everyone is smoking, you were considered odd not to. The languid girls propped on bar stools, wielding fabulously long cigarette holders, sipping at the latest exotic concoction prepared for them. The men all smart, sober suits, Brylcreemed hair and pencil moustaches.

Shaken not stirred – cocktail hour has arrived

This is the cocktail age, as much a part of the twenties scene as the Charleston and Flappers. Whilst cocktails have always been associated with the Savoy, they were being served across London as other hotels sought to cash in on the craze. In fact, strictly speaking, the cocktail was not a product of the twenties anyway. The first American bar was opened at the Criterion in 1878. They even imported Leo Engel, their own American bartender. The increasing popularity of American cocktails coincided with a major refit at the Savoy. In addition, the Savoy group rebuilt Claridges and added the Berkeley to its collection of hotels. All of them had American bars installed, but it was the Savoy's bar that outlasted them all and became a fixture in fashionable London.

The first high-profile barman to be employed by the Savoy was actually a woman. Ada Coleman started work in 1903 and she was still shaking until her retirement at the end of 1924. Her most famous concoction was the 'Hanky Panky', which was a mixture of gin, Italian vermouth, plus a couple of dashes of Fernet Branca. Robert Vermeire of the Embassy Club referred to 'Ada's Midnight Cocktail' in a 1922 book *Cocktails: How to Mix Them*.

Harry Craddock, an American, was appointed barman at the Savoy shortly after the advent of prohibition in the States. He is credited with the introduction of 'The White Lady'. He published the definitive *The Savoy Cocktail Book* in 1930 and it is still in print today. Although many of the cocktails were of his own creation, he also inherited a collection of recipes garnered by the hotel over forty years. He insisted that certain basic rules must be observed to create the perfect cocktail:

The starkly modern American Bar at The Savoy.

1. Ice is essential for almost all cocktails.
2. You must never use the same ice twice.
3. Whatever the ingredients, they mix better in a cocktail shaker.
4. Shake the shaker as hard as you can. As Harry Craddock said, 'You are trying to wake it up, not send it to sleep.'
5. If possible, ice the glasses before serving.
6. Drink the contents as soon as possible. 'Drink it whilst it's laughing at you'.

So now turn out your cupboards and dig out that old shaker and enjoy mixing just a few of those cocktails that were all the rage in the twenties.

Old Fashioned Cocktail

1 lump of sugar
2 dashes of angostura bitters
1 glass of rye or Canadian Club whisky

Crush the sugar and bitters together, add ice cube, decorate with a twist of lemon peel and slice of orange and stir well.

❈ ❈ ❈ ❈

Between The Sheets

1 dash lemon juice
$^1/_3$ brandy $^1/_3$ Cointreau $^1/_3$ Barcadi rum
Shake well and strain into cocktail glass.

❈ ❈ ❈ ❈

Side Car

$^1/_4$ lemon juice
$^1/_4$ Cointreau $^1/_3$ brandy

Shake well and strain into cocktail glass.

❈ ❈ ❈ ❈

35

The Barbary Coast Cocktail

$^1/_4$ gin $^1/_4$ Scotch whisky
$^1/_4$ Crème de cacao $^1/_4$ cream
Cracked ice

Serve in a highball glass.

❉ ❉ ❉ ❉

How about a prepared cocktail for bottling (it is suggested you speak to your bank manager first):

5 gallons of gin
2 gallons of water
1 quart of gomme syrup
2 ounces of orange peel
7 ounces of tincture of gentian
$^1/_2$ ounce of tincture of lemon peel

Mix together and give the desired colour with solferino and caramel in equal proportions

(Cocktail recipes reproduced courtesy of the Savoy Archive)

Below stairs

To enable guests to enjoy themselves, an army of workers had to beaver away below stairs in rather less luxurious surroundings. French kitchen workers were amazed at the quality of food they were allowed, after slaving over the hotel's stoves. In France, they tended to be fed from a communal stew, whilst at the Savoy they could fill themselves with beef steaks and mutton chops. Although the pay was poor, the working conditions hot and crowded, at least they had full stomachs. The chances of them growing fat, however, were negligible as they had to work long hours and at a frenetic pace. Pierre Hamp, in his book *Kitchen Prelude*, tells of working at a breathless speed. A diner's impatience could lead to instant dismissal. Speed and the greatest care in their work was demanded by the forerunners of Gordon Ramsay. These chefs were not celebrities, however, just masters of their craft.

At the Ritz the lower basement housed a staff kitchen as well as separate dining-rooms for waiters and valets. Porters and labourers were housed in their own dining area, as were the clerical staff. The lower ground floor contained the main kitchen, together with cool storage rooms. Stairs led up to the restaurant and down to the Banqueting Hall. A third staircase led to the Grill Room and private dining-rooms. Facing the kitchen was a large day cellar, with two sizeable racks for champagne. The larder entrance led to cold stores for game and meat. The ice room had built-in cold cupboards. At the Arlington Street end was the pastry room with two huge ovens. In addition to the kitchen staff, there was a vast range of fixtures and fittings to keep tabs on. Everything in the hotel, be it the furniture, linen or silverware, was of the highest quality. The silver plate collection was massive and weighed in at over five and a half tons. Cutlery was supplied by Christofle together with all the salt cellars, pepper grinders and sugar basins. Including tea and coffee pots, milk and water jugs, there were almost 20,000 pieces to keep in circulation. There were similar numbers of china, manufactured by Royal Doulton.

So whilst the hotel staff work away and the night shift arrives, our favoured guests take the lift to the upper floors to their comfortable suites with their pyjamas neatly laid out. The bed has been turned down displaying crisp, freshly laundered linen sheets and warm woollen blankets. In the bathroom the white pedestal washbasin is adorned with chunky, solid brass taps. The whole room is tiled from floor to ceiling in fashionable black and white. There is a wicker clothes basket for the day's discarded shirt and underwear. Just time for a shower, whose head is the size of a dinner plate. Refreshed, yet relaxed, it is time for our guest to sink down into bed, comforted by the goose-down pillows. Tomorrow will be another day for having a good time in London. Perhaps a little shopping or maybe a trip to the Queen's Club. Anyone for tennis?

PC George Scorey controlling the crowds at the 1923 FA Cup Final.

4

The Sporting Life

'I do love cricket – it's so very English.'

(Sarah Bernhardt)

Social division in sport during the 1920s truly reflected everyday life. Although the working man flocked weekly to watch his favourite football team or to pay a visit to the dog track, there were few activities where those from either side of the social spectrum competed directly against each other.

How's that? London's great cricket grounds

The major exception was cricket, which had been played in varying forms since the eighteenth century. Cricket was more than a game for the average Englishman. It was played at every school and it set out to teach the young about fair play. It was also thought to be very important in teaching British values to the 'natives' of the British Empire. Its status was emphasised in London by the existence of two iconic grounds – Lords and the Oval.

By 1920 – after the war – cricket in England was back in full swing. Lords was home to Middlesex in the county championship and was also an annual test match venue. Watching first-class cricket was a very different experience from the beer-driven chanting and the wearing of fancy dress favoured by today's spectators. Applause was confined to restrained clapping for exceptional play, otherwise total silence was expected during overs. Lords hosted three annual matches which underlined the social gap. The 'Gentlemen' versus 'Players' fixture dragged on until 1962. The distinction between the well-to-do amateurs (the Gentlemen) and the professionals (the Players) had been acknowledged since the game's very beginnings. In general, the toffs found bowling rather too arduous and it was probably a key factor in allowing working men to play alongside their 'betters', who preferred the art of batting. As the structure of the game developed, the professional was expected to help with ground maintenance and the cleaning of kit. This attitude had changed somewhat by the end of the Great War. Still, the amateurs were identified by their initials being printed before their surname on the printed scorecard, whilst those of the professionals came after. This distinction seems ludicrous today, but it probably spurred the Players on to win the fixture more often than not. Even when playing for the same team, the professionals had separate changing rooms. For the most part county players were poorly paid and it was only the few stars who began earning extra through endorsements and guest appearances.

So whilst the classes did integrate to some extent on the field, the divisions were further magnified by two other annual matches held at Lords. Eton versus Harrow and the Varsity match were major events in the social calendar. The Eton/Harrow meetings, particularly, were right up there with Ascot and Henley. Fashionable top-hatted men and their elegant ladies paraded in front of the pavilion during the luncheon break. The young boys from the schools were expected to wear top hats and stiff white collars.

Large crowds continued to follow county cricket in London. Lancashire and Yorkshire always provided stiff opposition, but it was Surrey who produced the major star of the twenties. Jack Hobbs in later life became the first working-class sportsman to be knighted. He fitted entirely the establishment's view of a perfect professional cricketer. His father had been a Cambridge University servant, so he knew his place. He was understated, unfailingly polite and always immaculately dressed. The war deprived him of the years when he would have been at the height of his powers, but he had the satisfaction of scoring his first century against Australia at the Oval, which helped to win the Ashes after a gap of fourteen years.

Crowds mingle in front of the pavilion at Lords during the Eton v Harrow match, one of the important social events of London's summer season.

The top professional at Middlesex was Patsy Hendren. During his career, he was second only to Jack Hobbs, scoring 170 centuries. He played in fifty-one test matches with a batting average of forty-seven. He was elected Cricketer of the Year in 1920. He suffered a loss of form the following year, but by 1923 he was again the scourge of the bowlers, amassing an amazing 3,000 runs. Although short in stature, he was at his best against fast bowling. A talented, all-round sportsman, he was still playing professional football for Brentford at the age of thirty-nine.

Billiards and snooker

Another game enjoyed by all sides of society was billiards, though rarely at the same table. Found in many of the capital's swankiest clubs as well as busy London pubs, the game enjoyed huge popularity during the twenties. Billiards had, supposedly, been imported from France, but was adopted by the British in the nineteenth century with the introduction of pockets rather than hoops. By the twenties, the slate-based table was well established, as were the rounded cue tips and the application of the all-important chalk. Whilst gentlemen repaired to the billiard room after supper, the hustlers were pocketing bets in pubs across London from gullible punters. The popularity of the game worried the Temperance Society and this led to a number of teetotal billiard halls being opened. Thurston Hall in Leicester Square became the home of professional billiards and snooker. Tom Newman dominated the billiards scene, winning the world title in 1921–22 and again between 1924 and 1927.

Snooker was developed in India during the Raj. Despite its rather aristocratic origins, it was seized upon and found favour in working men's clubs. The professional game was dominated from the mid-twenties by the Davis brothers, Fred and Joe. Joe was world champion from 1927 to 1940. At one time the brothers held both billiard and snooker titles.

42

Elite sports – from the croquet lawn to the shooting range

Perhaps the defining game for the gentry was croquet. Still many a fashionable London square resounded to the comforting sound of mallet on ball. There is still some doubt regarding its origins. A game called crookey, played in Ireland in the 1830s, may lay the strongest claim. Originally, the game's headquarters was at Wimbledon, but the popularity of tennis soon led to the croquet lawns being converted. The All England Croquet Club decamped to Hurlingham. Many a romance developed over a leisurely game and many of the 1920s' leading personalities became devotees, including Greta Garbo and Agatha Christie.

Riding, and particularly hunting, has always been associated with the aristocracy. All of London's hunting fields had gone by the 1920s, and riding was largely confined to being seen in Rotten Row. Originally built in the seventeenth century to provide a broad thoroughfare through Hyde Park to St James's Palace, it became increasingly a place for the well-to-do to be seen. Money now, rather than noble birth, dictated who trotted decorously down this most famous of bridle paths. Bankers, businessmen and even film stars paraded. This, to many traditionalists, was bad enough, but the regular arrival of the coloured entertainer Hutch caused a further deep intake of breath. They couldn't really criticize his appearance as he was always immaculate, from his hand-made boots to his silk top hat.

Although hockey in various forms can be traced back to the fourteenth century, we have to travel to nineteenth-century Blackheath to witness the birth of the modern game in England. The All Male Hockey Association was founded in 1886 and the clubs tended to be situated in the most affluent parts of London. With its popularity being spread by the British Army, the game had already become the national sport of India by 1920. In the same year, Britain won the gold medal at the Olympics, a task made easier by the fact that there were only four nations competing. Hockey, by the 1920s, was being played at all leading girls' schools. Mixed sex games also became popular and were known to be particularly vicious.

Polo is another socially elite game with military associations. Dating back hundreds of years to central Asia, the first recorded game in England took place on Hounslow Common in 1869. Rules were finalised in 1872 and two years later the Hurlingham Club assumed responsibility as the game's ruling body and, as such, became the sport's world headquarters. Due to the cost of maintaining a string of polo ponies, the sport was the most socially exclusive game played in London during the twenties. Great Britain again succeeded in winning gold in Antwerp, following it with a silver medal four years later in Paris.

For the most part, fencing also remained a socially exclusive sport, underlined by its military associations. It was taught at many public schools with St Paul's specialising in the discipline. The Regent Street Polytechnic (now the University of Westminster) was also a great supporter of the sport, with a very active women's section. In 1924, Gladys Davis won the silver medal in the individual foil event in Paris.

Shooting was also a popular activity with the ex-military establishment. At the beginning of the decade, there were a staggering 15,000 game-keepers employed across the country. The ever increasing urbanisation of London restricted the number of shoots available, leading to an exodus to the grouse moors during the season. Competition shooting, however, was gaining in popularity. Despite there being over twenty shooting titles at stake in the Antwerp Olympics (1920), Britain sent only seven competitors, none of whom won a medal.

Anyone for tennis?

Tennis is surely among the most social of games. Throughout London and the suburbs, lawn tennis clubs flourished. The game offered the perfect opportunity to meet members of the opposite sex in pleasant surroundings. Young ladies, wearing modest white skirts and opaque stockings, sit decorously sipping lemonade on Lloyd Loom chairs, whilst their white-flannelled boyfriends lounge over the railings of the wooden pavilion. There are shouts of 'jolly good shot' and 'oh, hard luck, darling'. This is English tennis, where the teas and the evening dance are almost more important than the game itself. It also provides a clue as to why, as a nation, the English have rarely been that successful at the top level. For most, the game was little more than pat-a-cake over the net, certainly in mixed doubles, where it was considered the height of rudeness for a man to serve hard to a lady. However, there were other wheezes used to gain an advantage.

> *'Though your game is hardly the best*
> *You can fray your opponent's nerves*
> *By methodically bouncing the ball*
> *At least ten times before your serves.'*

(Arnold J. Zarett)

Away from these provincial English clubs, tennis was a sport that created super stars. Glamorous men and women combined flashing backhand winners with grace and speed. The Wimbledon Championships have been held at the All England Club since 1877. In 1922, the old ramshackle, wooden-roofed arena was replaced by a huge new stadium that held up to 15,000 spectators. It was opened by King George V and many thought it would turn out to be a white elephant. In fact, the reverse was true and interest in the elite game mushroomed. It was a giant American, William Tilden, who took the sport on to a new level. He won the Wimbledon title in both 1920 and the following year, before winning again in 1930. He had the perfect physique, wide shoulders and long legs. The British players looked quite weedy standing alongside him. He was able to generate great power on both backhand and forehand wings from his wooden racquet. Admiration and adulation were showered on Tilden. The English blamed their lack of success on the ghastly climate, also claiming that participation rather than winning was what mattered, reflected in the nation's concentration on team games.

By 1926 the French had arrived. That year, Jean Barotra won Wimbledon and, along with René Lacoste, Jacques Brugnon and Henri Cochet, won the International Lawn Tennis Challenge (now known as the Davis Cup). Great though this generation of French players were, they failed always to impress the correspondent of the *Lawn Tennis and Badminton Magazine*. Of Barotra's 1925 semifinal with French compatriot Henri Cochet, he wrote: 'Cochet was volleying so poorly that he was almost afraid to go to the net. When Barotra gained a 3–1 lead in the next set, Cochet virtually curled up.' He wasn't too impressed by the final against Lacoste either. 'This match had its exciting episodes and its disturbing ones too. There were flashes of real greatness but the sustained brilliance of last year's final

Suzanne Lenglen seen here in action during the Wimbledon Ladies' Doubles Final of 1925. She brought style, excitement and even a little perspiration to the women's game.

46

was absolutely lacking.' As ever, British journalists could write the copy, but where were our players to throw down a challenge?

Stardom was not confined to the men's game. Whereas the Americans played to win, it was the French who were the crowd pleasers. The French girls pouted and shouted, the forerunners of today's outspoken players. Suzanne Lenglen first won Wimbledon in 1919. She went on to win the title six times, culminating in her 1925 victory when she lost only five games in the entire sequence of matches. Most of the games she won to love, thrashing poor Kitty McKane in the semifinal without losing a single game, and yet the English girl McKane was good enough to win Wimbledon twice herself. Lenglen, as well as being a superb player, was a trendsetter. She discarded the usual blouse and long skirt and played in a one-piece loose-fitting dress. Her short pleated skirt was copied by leading dress designers. She also wore a brightly coloured bandeau, which, again, became a fashion accessory much loved by the young. Lenglen had a game quite unlike any of the other leading ladies. She stretched herself physically in what some thought to be a most unladylike manner. She smashed, she volleyed and dived for seemingly lost causes. For heaven's sake, she sweated! Well, perspired anyway, and to cap it all she was capable of beating many of the leading men. Increasingly, she felt constrained by the pressure of constant travel. Also, whilst her appearances would boost the attendance of any tournament where she played, she was seeing very little personal financial return. In 1926, she turned professional with a view to cashing in on her popularity. Her professional career was short lived and she retired the following year to set up a tennis school near Roland Garros. To the All England Club, professionalism was against their whole ethos and they spitefully withdrew Lenglen's honorary membership.

The next superstar to arrive was the American Helen Wills. Known as 'Miss Poker Face', she rarely showed emotion on court. She was relentless in her search for success, which she achieved, surpassing Lenglen's record at Wimbledon by winning the championship eight times. Astonishingly, it was Kitty McKane who was the only player to beat her at Wimbledon, winning the title in 1924, 4–6, 6–4, 6–4. Wills generally wore an eye shade and, like Lenglen's bandeau, this became a sought-after accessory. More conventional than Lenglen, Wills continued to wear white stockings, as Queen Mary had let it be known that she hated seeing bare legs. King George's attitude to bare legs isn't recorded. In 1926, the royal family's interest in tennis was underlined when the future King George VI appeared in the men's doubles. There was a ray of hope for British men's tennis with the emergence of a young Cambridge undergraduate. Bunny Austin reached the semifinals of the men's doubles in 1926. It was in the thirties that he really became a world force and a trendsetter by being the first man to wear shorts at Wimbledon. Hopefully, Queen Mary had become a convert by then.

If lawn tennis was considered the preserve of the middle classes, then real tennis was the ultimate in elitism. Real or royal tennis is the game from which lawn tennis was derived. Dating back centuries to continental Europe, it is thought to have been played originally with the palm of the hand and later with a glove. Its popularity was restricted as large indoor courts were required in custom-constructed buildings. As such, participation was confined to a privileged few. The venues available in London underline this. The Royal Tennis Court at Hampton Court is the oldest surviving venue in England, but it was also possible to play at Lords or Queen's Club, if you had the right connections.

Boaters, blazers and bridges

Joining Wimbledon as one of London's great social events was the annual Royal Regatta at Henley. Never mind that your rowing experience only extended to a spin on the Serpentine, you just had to be seen there sporting a boater and blazer. However, it was the other great annual sporting event held on the Thames that really captured Londoners' attention. The Varsity Boat Race from Putney to Mortlake saw the tow-paths and bridges packed with raucous spectators, sporting rosettes of light or dark blue. Many came from the poorest areas and allegiances were often split between families. The twenties was a particularly lean period for Oxford who only recorded one victory over the decade in 1923. They experienced a sinking feeling two years later as foul weather left them waterlogged. They had drawn the Surrey station, which had left them exposed to high winds and a heavy swell.

Out on the fairway – social climbing on the golf course

'Golf is so popular simply because it is the
best game in the world at which to be bad.'

(A. A. Milne)

Social pretension tended to create its own elitism when attempting to join one of London's golf clubs. Golfing skill was far less important than your connections. Whilst, undoubtedly, romances flourished on the fairways, as they did at tennis clubs, golf offered more commercial opportunities. The golf course was a place where useful contacts could be made and business discreetly discussed. So it was important to be proposed and seconded for membership before being interviewed to see if you passed muster.

The golf club became an important centre for the well-to-do middle class. It was a game with wide appeal. You didn't have to be young. You didn't have to be fit. For married couples, it was a game that could be enjoyed together. The golf club was also a place to take a convivial drink after an arduous round. Then, perhaps, a relaxing game of billiards, whilst the ladies played a few hands of bridge. You were made to feel important at your club. The professional and the steward were always suitably deferential and you were able to mix with the type of people you felt comfortable with. The club secretary tended to be a dependable ex-military type who saw to the upholding of standards at the club. Life was good, you felt cocooned in a safe, familiar world. Not if you were Jewish, though. Although rarely outwardly admitted, anti-Semitism was rife. Perhaps this was just an extension of the general suspicion of 'foreignness' at the time. The fact is, many of London's golf clubs barred Jews. This led to several Jewish courses being formed, including Hartsbourne, Bushey in 1928.

Whilst being appointed captain of a golf club was considered a great honour, it was an expensive one. The captain was expected to provide competition prizes, pay for trips to other clubs and host dinners. Only the wealthy could contemplate taking on the responsibilities. Some clubs began to allow artisan membership. This was open to club servants, caddies and local tradesmen. For reduced fees they were allowed to play at restricted times, though this did not always include admittance to the club house.

Rugby

Mention London sport and you tend to end up back at Blackheath. The Blackheath Football Club ('The Club') claims to be the first English rugby club. By the 1920s, most leading schools had opted for 'rugger' rather than the round ball game. Many of the clubs playing then still flourish today under the professional code. Perhaps the most famous, Harlequins, started life as Hampstead Football Club but, as players were recruited from further afield, a more appropriate name was sought. They decided on Harlequins and, in turn, settled on the famous quartered shirt, whose design has been hijacked and reinvented in different colours as a modern fashion item. Harlequins traditionally recruited players from influential backgrounds, which earned them the tag of 'the fancy Dans' of the game. Many of their players enjoyed even more success off than on the pitch. Saracens are also still playing in the top flight of the modern game, as are Wasps, whose black and gold striped socks represent their original strip. London also supported three 'exile' teams: London Irish, London Scottish and London Welsh. This provided opportunities for the legions of people who had left these countries to get together at the weekend. For the most part, people tended not to move so far away from the area where they were brought up, and so old boys' rugby clubs were flourishing, many fielding as many as seven or eight teams. This meant that boys who had recently left school were often thrown together with hardy fifty-year-olds who refused to accept the passing of time. The modern game requires a far greater level of fitness, but in those days an overweight prop forward could shine in the scrum and rumble round the pitch quite happily, whilst the 'pretty boys' in the backs could get the glory. Then it was into the communal bath, where latecomers had to part the scum before getting out dirtier than when they got in. After drying off it was into the bar for a few pints. It was, apparently, unwise to take a girlfriend to watch you play, unless you were sure of her absolute devotion to you, as there was always some smooth 'lounge lizard' waiting to move in.

Whilst the top games in the twenties were very competitive, there were no official leagues or knock-out cups. Fixture lists tended to pitch the same teams against each other every season, with relatively little change. Local derbies were fought with added ferocity. The highlight for most teams was the traditional Easter tour. This remained a hazy memory for many, with heroic amounts of beer being consumed, and yet, the following day, the team would be ready for another match. The tours of Wales were reportedly particularly painful, with many of the London-based clubs being trounced. Rugby in the valleys was played with a unique brand of skill and ferocity that few who were on the receiving end forgot.

Twickenham was already the home of English rugby and played host to internationals and the annual Varsity match. During the war, the ground had been used for grazing and it was in 1921 that King George V unveiled the war memorial, the same year that Oxford beat Cambridge 11–5. England had beaten France in the first international played after the war and in 1924 went on to win the Grand Slam, beating Scotland at Twickenham 19–0. By 1925, the north stand had extended the capacity to 60,000, and later that year Cyril Brownlie of the All Blacks became the first player to be sent off for overly violent play in an international. This didn't stop New Zealand extending their unbeaten record, winning the match 17–11.

Soccer – the beautiful game in the big city

'The rules of soccer are very simple, basically, it is this:
If it moves, kick it. If it doesn't, kick it until it does.'

(Phil Woosnam)

From Craven Cottage to Highbury, huge crowds of cloth-capped Londoners flocked to support their local teams each Saturday. Even amateur clubs drew crowds that would be the envy of many lesser professional clubs today. By 1920, football had become the working man's sport as much as beer was his drink. Banks of supporters with rattles and scarves cheered from the terraces. It was a family game. Youngsters were passed and lifted aloft all the way to the front so they could enjoy a better view. There was no obscene chanting and little swearing, but still the atmosphere was normally highly charged, yet good humoured.

Football drew massive crowds during the 1920s, few more so than Chelsea, seen here playing Aston Villa at a packed Stamford Bridge.

On the pitch the players wore long, baggy shorts and heavy leather boots that came up over their ankles to offer extra protection. The goalkeeper wore a thick, woollen polo-necked sweater. This was not a game for prima donnas. There were no dramatic dives and feigning injuries. This was a man's game of real physical contact. The leather ball became so heavy during wet conditions that it took strength as well as skill to move it any distance. It was a game of crunching tackles and hefty shoulder charges. It was quite common for a goalkeeper to be barged into his own net as he attempted to reach a cross. Although the crowds were huge the players were poorly paid. Rather than turn up at the ground in a Ferrari, they were more likely to arrive with the fans on a bus.

In 1920, the professional league was extended to forty-four clubs with the addition of the third division (south). London clubs can often trace their origins back to church or works teams. Support was almost tribal. The East Enders supported West Ham or Leyton Orient, whilst further north the rosettes and scarves showed allegiance to Arsenal or Tottenham Hotspur. To the west, Fulham, Chelsea, Brentford and Queen's Park Rangers were cheered on. All those clubs survive and some have become famous worldwide. During the twenties it was the northern and midlands teams that tended to dominate. Not a single London club won the first division title during the whole decade. In 1921, Tottenham Hotspur did manage to win the FA Cup. The post-war venue for the event had been Crystal Palace, but the army had taken it over and so the match was played at Stamford Bridge. Chelsea's ground was considered to be the most modern stadium in London at the time. By today's standards it would have been judged uncomfortable and dangerous. The majority stood packed on terraces open to the elements protected from crushing by a few crash barriers. The seating was largely confined to hard wooden benches. The gents' toilets were constructed of corrugated iron cladding and bare earth. Matters were made worse that day by torrential rain. The pitch was little more than a quagmire. Newly promoted Tottenham had become known for their constructive play, with an emphasis on dribbling. The conditions made this impossible. Having triumphed over a strong Aston Villa side in the semifinal, they were favourites to beat second division Wolverhampton Wanderers. The weather acted as a great leveller and there had been little chance of a goal for either side by half time. The crowd was drenched and disappointed. The Wolverhampton team changed their soaked shirts during the interval. The replacement strip didn't have the town's crest on the shirts and, bizarrely, it was to this oversight that their defeat was attributed. Tottenham's single goal victory was a rare moment of glory for London clubs during the 1920s.

The 1922 Cup Final was also won by a single goal when Huddersfield defeated Preston North End at Stamford Bridge. This match was poorly attended and was, therefore, thought to have contributed to the chaotic scenes at the first match played at Wembley Stadium in 1923. For over forty years, Wembley had been associated with leisure activities. There were cricket and football pitches laid out alongside well-maintained walkways and formal gardens. Due to its popularity, at the end of the nineteenth century it was decided to connect the site to central London with the introduction of a linking railway line. After the war, the government set out ambitious plans to hold a British Empire exhibition. The centrepiece was to be a national stadium. With over 200 acres Wembley was considered an ideal site. Initially, it was planned for the stadium to have a capacity of 125,000 with seating for 30,000. This was amended to 90,000 and the new Empire Stadium, as it was known, was completed in less than a year, at a cost of £750,000. It was a showpiece, the largest and most up-to-date stadium in the world. By the end of the exhibition, over 5 million visitors had viewed the state-of-the-art stadium.

The 1923 Cup Final could easily have ended in disaster. The poor attendance the previous year wrong-footed the authorities. There was even talk of the stadium being something of a white elephant. However, 90,000 tickets had been sold and a trouble-free match was anticipated. In the event, because West Ham had reached the final, the turnstiles were overwhelmed. Hordes of East End fans joined the ticket holders, breaking through the barriers and spilling onto the pitch. The crowd was frighteningly out of control. People, including police, were crushed or trampled on. There were over fifty quite serious injuries but, amazingly, nobody was killed. It took over half an hour for mounted police to restore some sort of order. It was PC George Scorey who became the hero of the hour. He was largely responsible, mounted on his white horse, for gradually getting the mob back beyond the touchline. Today, of course, the match would have been abandoned. Bolton went on to beat West Ham 2–0, but it is the policeman on the white horse for which the match is mostly remembered.

International football was largely confined to matches against the home nations. Every other year London was invaded by over 30,000 marauding Scots. Many, kilted and accompanied by bagpipes, came to do battle with 'the old enemy'. Londoners not interested in football looked on in alarm. London rivalries were forgotten as the fans mingled with thousands brought in by train from all corners of the country. Even though they tended to outnumber the Scots by two to one, the English were still unable to rival the passion and noise of their cousins from north of the border. Football was the great moving force for the working man. It offered an escape from what, for many, were boring, repetitive jobs. It was so influential that production levels in factories ebbed and flowed with the results of local teams.

Bowls please

After the excitement and emotion of the match on a Saturday, a game of bowls the following afternoon could help lower the blood pressure. The ancient game was enjoying a surge of popularity. Many local councils laid down bowling greens in their parks. The more enlightened large employers also provided facilities, as did Conservative and working men's clubs. The game had the great advantage of being affordable and open to both sexes. It could also be played to an advanced level in old age. Like tennis and cricket, it also offered social advantages. Picture a sunny afternoon with the white-clad bowlers bent in concentration, whilst on the terrace of the wooden pavilion others enjoy a traditional English afternoon tea.

It's a knock-out – boxing punches above its weight

Even in boxing it was impossible to ignore the social divide. Here was the ultimate sport where the well-to-do watched, whilst poor young men knocked each other senseless. This was the sport offering those from the most deprived backgrounds the opportunity to break away and not only to find fame, but also to become stinking rich. The National Sporting Club, situated in King Street, Covent Garden, provided a strange backdrop to this skilful, yet violent sport. At the beginning of the twenties, boxing formed a type of after dinner cabaret for the members. Unlike at any other venue the bouts were fought in total silence. The dinner-jacketed patrons looked on, puffing at their cigars, and if the fight pleased them they would toss a few coins in the ring to help swell the contestants' earnings. These 'nobbings' were a part of boxing folklore and the practice extended to the small halls and boxing booths throughout the country. Most fighters started boxing as amateurs at one of the many clubs in London, such as the famous Repton Club. Most could not wait to turn pro and earn some money. Famously, London policeman Harry Mallin remained an amateur. He won an Olympic gold medal in 1920 and became the first Briton to successfully defend his title four years later in Paris. He retired in 1928, having remained undefeated after 300 bouts.

Professional boxing is to many a barbaric sport. However, it demands fitness, strength, bravery and skill. Historically, it has always attracted racial minorities, immigrants recently arrived in this country. In the twenties there was a succession of Jewish fighters from the East End. The Star of David was a common sight on fighters' shorts. These were the children of parents who worked in the sweatshops of a strange country. They grew up tough, knowing how to handle themselves. They fought at rowdy venues: Premierland on Commercial Road in Stepney, or at Manor Hall in Mare Street, Hackney. They won their respect across London, at Paddington Baths, the Stadium Club in Holborn or The Ring on Blackfriars Road. Although generally conforming to the Queensberry Rules, these venues were bear pits. Fighters were allowed to take fearsome punishment, which would not be tolerated today. The sport became better regulated with the formation of the British Boxing Board of Control in 1929, but

After a plentiful supper, members sat in silence at the National Sporting Club watching the boxers. If the contest pleased them they would toss a few coins and an odd note into the ring in appreciation, known as 'nobbings'.

gambling ensured that criminals were never far away. Fight fixing was not uncommon. Cuts inflicted by the fighter's own second, with a judicious nick of a razor, could bring about an unexpected result. This type of incident frequently led to crowd disorder. There was often more money to be made by a boxer for throwing a fight than by his modest purse.

While most fought with little rest between bouts, and could end up battered and punch-drunk, a few really talented fighters became stars and role models for the next generation. The first London Jewish fighter to achieve international fame was Ted 'Kid' Lewis. He was born Gershon Mendeloff in Aldgate in 1893. He turned pro at sixteen as a featherweight. He spent the war years in the States, returning to London in 1919 as a welterweight. During his time in America he won the world title before losing it in the last of a protracted series of bouts against the American Jack Britton. Back in London he won the British and European titles, beating the aptly named Johnny Basham. His weight continued to increase and he soon relinquished the title before winning the middleweight division in 1921. The following year, he challenged Georges Carpentier, the world light heavyweight champion. Carpentier was suave, good-looking and had a reputation for being something of a playboy. Perhaps this encouraged Lewis to think that he could concede two stones in weight. Lewis was a skilful and aggressive fighter and for most of the first round he was all over the Frenchman. He was giving him a boxing lesson. As the round came to a close, the referee pulled Lewis away to warn him about holding. Looking towards the referee, Lewis lost concentration for a second. That's all it took. Taking advantage, Carpentier flashed in a vicious right hook. Lewis crashed to the canvas and took the full count. Pandemonium. The crowd was furious. They had expected a long, close fight. They felt cheated and so did Lewis, but he said he didn't bear Carpentier a grudge. He was a great fighter with a swarming, all-action style, but he was not very good with money. Although he had earned a fortune in the States, most of it had gone by the time of his retirement. One of Britain's all-time greats, he died in obscurity in a home for aged Jews in Clapham in 1970. His is a familiar tale of boxers who make a fortune but fail to hang onto it.

Poverty acted as a great stimulus for a generation of Jewish fighters from the East End. Another all-time great was Jack 'Kid' Berg, born Judah Bergman in 1909, and known as 'The Whitechapel Whirlwind' for his non-stop machine-gun style of fighting. He exploded on the world scene, like Lewis, on his first visit to the States, when he defeated the highly rated Pedro Amador. Americans were always sceptical about British fighters. They tended to box in a conventional, upright stance behind a straight left. Berg's style was quite the opposite. He bulldozed opponents in what some described as a demented attack. He went on to win other bouts before being held to a draw by Billy Petrolle, who was known as 'The Fargo Express'. Within a month, they had a re-match. Berg had not recovered from the effects of the last fight. Petrolle overwhelmed the East End boy, sending him to the canvas a sickening eleven times, before he was finally knocked out in the fifth round. The Americans declared 'The Kid' to be just another in a long line of British 'horizontal chumps'. This was underlined when Berg was beaten by Spug Myers, with a horrendous low blow.

Berg returned to London to pick up the pieces of his career. He soon won the British lightweight title by beating Alf Mancini in fifteen rounds. By 1929, Berg had won four more bouts in England and felt confident enough to try his luck in the States once more. He fought an amazing eighteen times that year, winning all but one bout, which ended in a draw. By 1930, the 'Whitechapel Whirlwind' had become world champion by beating Mushy Callahan, and became immortalised in East End folklore. Never far from the headlines, he had a well publicised affair with the film star, Mae West. After retirement, he was associated with the gangland boss, Jack Spot, who had been a childhood neighbour.

Another East End fighter (though not Jewish) was Bombardier Billy Wells, who was born in Cable Street in 1889. He joined the Royal Artillery when he was eighteen, and it was due to his rank of bombardier that he carried the name throughout his career. His finest days were before the war, when he became the first heavyweight to win the Lonsdale Belt defending his British title fourteen times. He saw service in the war and was promoted to sergeant. He resumed his career after the war, defending his title successfully against Joe Beckett, before losing in a re-match. As often happens in the fight game, Wells continued boxing, although he was already past his best. He fought on until 1925, losing as many bouts as he won. He had a successful retirement, publishing a book on modern boxing. His second source of fame came as the muscle man with the gong in J. Arthur Rank's film productions.

On track – the race is on for the latest craze

'I thought of that while riding my bike.'

(Albert Einstein on the Theory of Relativity)

Cycling, as a leisure pursuit, became a craze in the 1920s. With still relatively little motor traffic, it didn't take long for Londoners to reach the leafy suburbs and the open country beyond. Whole families would go off for the day with their picnics stowed carefully away in wicker panniers. For young men, drop handlebars became almost a fashion statement. Britain has always excelled in track and velodrome racing. During the 1920s, the sport reached its height of popularity with 10,000 regularly attending the Good Friday meeting at the Herne Hill track in south London. Lewis Meredith was an early star, appearing in three Olympics, including the 1920 event when he was thirty-eight.

Imported from the States, the introduction of greyhound racing unleashed a tidal wave of interest for the working man. The Greyhound Racing Association was formed in 1925 and the first stadium was developed in Manchester. The sport enjoyed phenomenal success and within two years it was estimated that over 4 million people passed through the turnstiles. In 1927, the Association acquired the almost derelict White City Stadium. Soon there were eighteen tracks operating across the country, witnessing the fastest growth of spectators of any British sport. Horse racing might be the preserve of the 'nobs', but greyhounds allowed the working man the opportunity to back his fancy in surroundings and company he felt comfortable with. Most of London's tracks were situated in heavily populated locations and, as racing tended to be at night, so it was easy to go along after work. Betting took place with on-course bookmakers, as the tote didn't start operating until 1930. The White City Stadium was built for the Franco-British exhibition of 1908. During the Great War, like many London stadia, it had been used by the army. By 1926, it had fallen into a dreadful state of disrepair. Under the watchful eye of General Critchley of the Greyhound Racing Association, it was restored and even included the first restaurant to be opened in a London stadium. The inaugural meeting attracted over 10,000 and soon crowds estimated to be well in excess of 30,000 were attending. London's love affair with greyhound racing was to last for another thirty years, and it has now reinvented itself to appeal to a modern audience, albeit on a lesser scale.

Speedway's popularity ran alongside greyhound racing and the sport shared many of the same venues. It was natural that the emergence of motorcycles on the road would lead to the introduction of an organised sport. It promised thrills and spills as powerful 500cc bikes competed on cinder tracks, with no brakes. Teams were formed and the races pitched two from each side against each other. It was only at the end of the decade that properly organised events got underway, with leagues being formed in 1929. London newspapers were quick to see the crowd-pleasing potential and, together with some of the national papers, offered sponsorship. Huge crowds were attracted to tracks, including White City, Stamford Bridge and West Ham. The acrid smells and rasping engines hit a nerve with Londoners as massive crowds attended a sport which was to gain further popularity during the 1930s.

Down the boozer – darts takes flight

Darts, along with cribbage, dominoes and shove-halfpenny, would have been played in almost every London pub back in the 1920s. Today, the constant search for profit has all but banished them from most establishments. Darts, however, has emerged as a popular, modern sport. Its origins can be traced back to medieval England. It is thought that shortened arrows were thrown at the bottom of empty wine barrels. Even in those far off days, the connection of drink with darts existed. The game then developed with a section of tree being substituted for the wine barrel. As the wooden board dried out, cracks appeared in segments, this became the forerunner of the board we know today. The modern game of darts was created in 1926. A group of London brewery men formed the National Darts Association. It was a year earlier that the Southwark brewery, Barclay, Perkins & Co., formed the earliest sponsored darts league. By 1930, every London brewery had a darts league. The game helped bring customers into the pubs on a regular basis and create an atmosphere that today, unfortunately, has largely been lost. As with other sports, darts offered the working man quality recreation time without breaking the bank. In 1927, the *News of the World* sponsored its first individual darts championship, with contestants restricted to those living within the Metropolitan area.

For the first time, social change ensured that even the humblest in the land had some leisure time. All across London, those who previously had been subjected to a life of endless work and drudgery could begin to enjoy themselves – and they did!

5

The Silver Screen

'*Who the heck wants to hear actors talk?*'

(Harry Warner)

Whilst the Bright Young People were either careering around London in the latest limousines or languidly sipping cocktails, ordinary Londoners were doing what the British do best, queuing. Not for buses or trams. Not at the butchers or bakers. No, they were queuing with a sense of anticipation and excitement to see their favourite stars at 'the pictures'. They stood in the rain and fog and then the audience from one viewing was eagerly replaced by the waiting crowd. Although there had been films to see before the war, now the moving picture represented, perhaps for the first time, mass entertainment. You could thrill to the endless adventures of Pearl White in the weekly serial *The Perils of Pauline*. At the end of each episode the intrepid star was left in dire danger. Struggling vainly, she raised her pretty face as she lay prone, tied to a railway track as an express train roared towards her. In the darkness of the back row the amorous young man could draw his frightened girlfriend towards him. Where else in crowded London could young lust develop without prying eyes? It wasn't only the film performance that offered excitement.

The cinema offered an escape from the humdrum existence of every day life. It allowed the audience to dream, to be transported to a world few knew existed. Ornate picture palaces rose in the West End. They had vast, glamorous foyers and commissionaires dressed in uniforms befitting some Ruritanian prince. Inside the auditorium, there were plush seats with ashtrays handy. For the young this was heaven, for their parents it was an affordable social event.

One of the grandest London cinemas was the Empire in Leicester Square, built on the site of the theatre bearing the same name. Opening in November 1928, it seated an astonishing 3,000 and featured a massive Wurlitzer organ. Not all the picture houses were so imposing, many being converted from dingy, existing buildings, which became known as 'flea pits'.

It was around Leicester Square, The Haymarket and Regent Street that the most prestigious cinemas were clustered. The richly decorated Plaza in Lower Regent Street opened in 1926. The Haymarket, meanwhile, saw the Carlton, followed by the Capitol in 1928, helping to satisfy the seemingly insatiable demand for Londoners to be entertained.

The New Gallery in Regent Street had formerly exhibited contemporary paintings and photographs. It was converted into a popular cinema seating 800 and, initially, had the largest cinema orchestra in London. The emergence of the 'talkies' led to a further extension to a 1,400 capacity. As well as blockbusters, it showed foreign films on Sundays which drew in capacity audiences. With both Paramount and Universal building super-sized cinemas in 1923, Lower Regent Street continued to be a centre for cinema goers.

The suburbs were not only home to the early British film studios at Elstree and Ealing, but also saw the emergence of some of the country's most extravagant cinemas. One of the grandest was the Granada in Tooting, whose architecture was based on the Alhambra Palace in Granada. The Elephant and Castle Trocadero housed a mighty Wurlitzer, as did the Astoria at Finsbury Park. Picture palaces were appearing in increasing numbers throughout suburbia. Bermondsey was not alone in offering a variety of choices covering the Rialto, the Trocette, the Stork and the Grand. There was to be no turning back. Cinema was taking a central place in London's popular culture.

The early days of film were dominated by the massive Hollywood studios, which were churning out upwards of 800 films a year. Right from the beginning they introduced the studio system, which tied their chosen stars into lengthy contracts. As the industry developed during the twenties, casting, production and distribution were all controlled by the studio. The industry was dominated by a handful of massive organisations. Metro-Goldwyn-Mayer was formed in 1924, a year after Warner Bros. Famous Players-Lasky Corporation became

Ronald Colman, the English 'Valentino' who became successful in Hollywood playing both romantic and adventurous roles.

Even 'the world's sweetheart', as she was known, found the transition to sound movies to be her undoing. For a time during the early twenties Mary Pickford was reckoned to be the most famous woman on the planet.

Paramount Studios in 1927, whilst RKO was evolved from the Mutual Film Corporation in 1928. Fox Film Corporation was known as Fox Movietone News before eventually becoming 20th-Century Fox in 1935. These influential concerns had massive production studios, with the capacity to create their own elaborate sets. They also went on to buy many of their own cinemas, thus controlling their entire output. The Empire in Leicester Square was owned by Metro-Goldwyn-Mayer.

This claustrophobic control led to a group of stars forming their own breakaway company. Douglas Fairbanks, Mary Pickford, Charlie Chaplin and D. W. Griffith formed United Artists as early as 1919, thus giving them total artistic and financial control. The British film industry did its best to compete, but was hampered by a lack of finance. One of our first home-grown stars was Ronald Colman, who appeared in several of Cecil Hepworth's Pioneer productions. Colman had debonair looks with fine, aquiline features. It was not long before he was off to Hollywood and by 1923 he had the leading role in *The White Sister*, starring opposite Lilian Gish. Douglas Fairbanks, who had already proved his business acumen by breaking away from the major studios, continued to be the leading American heartthrob. He was usually cast in swashbuckling parts and Londoners flocked to see him appear with Mary Pickford, who was known as 'The World's Sweetheart'. They were married in 1920 following quickie divorces. His wedding gift to his bride was a huge mansion in Beverley Hills. This set the precedent for stars in the decades to come, buying lavish homes and generally flaunting their wealth.

The British aristocracy thought this awfully common and it confirmed their view that money in the wrong hands would prove extremely damaging to society as a whole. The rest of the population couldn't care less. They fed off the crumbs of information given to them by the publicity departments of the leading studios. The world of celebrity was embraced and revered.

The producers of films became ever more ambitious. Drama and comedy were joined by the Hollywood epic. *Ben-Hur* starred the Mexican actor, Ramón Novarro. He had legions of adoring fans and was presented as a rival to possibly the greatest of the early screen legends, Rudolph Valentino.

Rudolph Valentino

Born of a French mother and Italian father, Valentino became the undisputed sex symbol of his day – a forerunner to pop stars. His appearance on screen could produce mass hysteria and yet contemporary

A rare, intimate, domestic photograph of screen idol, Rudolph Valentino, taken shortly before his premature death in 1926.

accounts of meeting him in person make him sound rather unprepossessing. He appears to have been like many fashion models who only come alive when placed in front of a camera. Eddie Marsh on meeting Valentino at a dinner party mistook him for a waiter. He described him as 'the ugliest man at the table, without a particle of charm'. It was surely a jealousy thing. Many British men were said to hate Valentino (probably because he was everything they were not). He was not overtly masculine but he oozed sex appeal. He danced the tango as no one had danced it before. Beverley Nichols, the writer, had a theory, quoted in Alan Jenkins' book *The Twenties*, that women lusted after Valentino because he treated them so badly. Certainly on film he hurled them around rather and once in a while smacked their bottoms. From this rather scant evidence, Nichols came up with the rather bizarre theory that these newly emancipated women were attracted to masochism and really wanted to be raped. As a life-long homosexual, it seemed unlikely that he had any particular insight into the female psyche, but who can tell?

It was for the silent film, *The Sheik*, made in 1921 that Valentino is best remembered. Although only small in stature, he plays the 'he man', carrying a silently screaming and struggling Agnes Ayres to his tent and flinging her on the bed. She is all wide-eyed and innocence incarnate; the caption on screen reads, 'Why have you brought me here?' The audience knows the answer... Although he made many other successful films, moving from studio to studio to increase his already heady earnings, it was *The Sheik* that captured Valentino's essential magnetism.

His death, at the early age of thirty-one in 1926, produced an outpouring of public grief, a foretaste of similar scenes brought about by the death of Princess Diana. He died of peritonitis having been diagnosed with a perforated ulcer. For days the front pages of the British press had no room for any other news. On 23rd August the *Daily Express* reported his condition was critical with doctors at his bedside. He died that day and the world was stunned. Rumours, circulated later, offered wild theories, including that he had been taking drugs to stem accelerating hair loss. On 25th August the *Express* reported that Valentino was lying in state in New York. His body was embalmed and lay in a silver and bronze casket with a glass top.

Many women became hysterical and it was reported that some had even committed suicide. There were reports of rioting as crowds waited to view his body. It is reckoned they need not have bothered as the body was supposedly only that of a wax dummy substituted due to fears that the crowd would become uncontrollable. Flags flew at half mast. Over 100,000 turned out as the cortège made its way to St Malachy's church. Even then the drama was not over. Actress Pola Negri prostrated herself before the coffin. Four black-shirted stooges stood guard whilst, supposedly, a wreath had been sent by Benito Mussolini. Later it was claimed that the fascist element had been laid on as a publicity stunt by the studio. Why? Was the body really a dummy? Nothing is certain except that in London groups of young women were reported to be inconsolable.

Kings of comedy

Meanwhile, the cameras continued to roll. During the silent film era, comedy was proving even more popular than drama. It still retains a timeless quality. Just witness youngsters today watching Laurel and Hardy or Buster Keaton, whereas silent drama films appear to be hammy and overacted. Comedy stars had risen to be amongst the highest paid with Charlie Chaplin reputed to be pocketing $4,000 a week.

Even at this early stage of film development, scandal was seldom far away. At a party given to celebrate Fatty Arbuckle's astonishing one-million-dollar, three-year contract with Paramount, disaster struck. Virginia Rappe, a twenty-six-year-old example of an early groupie, died in suspicious circumstances. There was talk of dark deeds and rape. Arbuckle was eventually charged with murder. There were two retrials before he was eventually cleared, but very real suspicion remained about his involvement. Despite several attempted comebacks, his career was effectively ruined. No set-backs, however, no matter how sordid, could stop the forward march of the film industry. Popular culture was born and the British public were fed snippets of information through the newspapers and specialist magazines.

The silent comedy stars were quite brilliant at conveying the plot by what was, in effect, miming. The film was normally accompanied by a mighty organ or piano. The player would match the accompaniment to the plot unfolding on the screen. The era produced an outstanding array of comic talent, including the Keystone Cops, Ben Turpin, Harold Lloyd, Buster Keaton and, of course, Charlie Chaplin.

Charlie Chaplin

Like so many Hollywood stars, Chaplin was born in England. Unfashionable Walworth was the starting point for possibly the greatest comic actor the screen has produced. He went to America in his early teens, finding work with Keystone Studios in the early 1900s. It was during this period that he began to perfect the tramp character that was initially to make his name. Silence was truly golden for the comedy actors because their work was instantly universal and, as such, easy to sell to non English-speaking markets. The tramp character had the unrivalled appeal of the poor down-trodden man overcoming the might of wealth and authority.

Like Chaplin, Stan Laurel was born in England and, as such, was held a favourite with British audiences. He had acted as an understudy to Chaplin when he joined Fred Karno's Troupe touring America in 1910. By the mid-twenties he saw his future mainly in writing with the Hal Roach Comedy Studios. A quirk of fate led to the forming of his partnership with American Oliver Hardy. An injury to an actor due to appear in a film with Hardy led to Stan Laurel deputising. It was 1927 and one of cinema's iconic film partnerships was formed. The two became great friends and the rapport transmitted itself through to their countless performances. Their transition from silent films to the 'talkies' appeared effortless and their popularity continued to grow. By the end of the era they had become the film industy's favourite double act.

In August 1921 Evelyn Waugh went to see Chaplin in *The Kid*. 'I confess I was disappointed with it,' he wrote. 'It was too self-conscious and sentimental. The part I liked best was that in which he was most like his old knockabout films. He did a splendid fight with a brick which cheered me a lot.' He seemed to view Harold Lloyd rather more positively. His diary for September 1926 states,

Laurel and Hardy's comedy still manages to travel well across generations. Stan Laurel, like many Hollywood stars, was born in England and cut his teeth in British music hall before going to Hollywood.

'Went to see the new Harold Lloyd film *For Heaven's Sake*. I found it excellent, contrary to most reports. In the evening I drank brandy at the Kit Kat Club.'

Goodbye silence – hello talkies...

Like Chaplin, Lloyd was successful in developing his career after the introduction of the talkies. A. P. Herbert was obviously having an off day when he wrote in *Punch* that the talkies were 'doomed to an early, but expensive, death'. At one stage it seemed as if he might be right. The Warner Brothers almost went bankrupt when they decided to introduce the Vitaphone disc. All the other major studios had rejected this new piece of technology. Warners ploughed on producing a film starring John Barrymore. This was a swashbuckling version of *Don Juan* with synchronised music played by the New York Philarmonic. The discs were played whilst the film was being projected. Although the film appeared to be a box office success, the investment required was huge and it was rated a financial failure. *Don Juan* featured only the musical score and sound effects but no dialogue. However, it was Warners' next major production *The Jazz Singer* that made history. It catapulted the movie industry forward to become the major player in the field of entertainment for generations to come. It was the movie that was to consign the silent film to the bin. The première of *The Jazz Singer* must have been extremely tense. The technology was complicated and, although the film ran for less than forty minutes, there were fifteen film reels and discs to be co-ordinated. The show had been a hit on Broadway, but its star George Jessell, and then Eddie Cantor, had turned down the leading role. Luckily, Al Jolson, who the Warners also thought would reject them, was intrigued that the story related to the son of a synagogue cantor, which actually mirrored his own background. Did Jolson's excitement get the better of him as the cameras began to roll or was the whole thing planned? As the orchestra struck up to play the first number 'Toot Toot Tootsie Goodbye', Jolson appeared to interrupt, speaking out to the audience: 'Wait a minute, wait a minute, I tell yer, you ain't heard nothin' yet'. The talking pictures had arrived.

John Gilbert, seen here with Renée Adorée, was one of the silent-screen stars who failed to make the transition into the 'talkies'.

The other studios panicked, cancelling planned films or hurriedly getting scripts written. Sound offered endless opportunities. The film musical was waiting in the wings. The sound of gunfire was soon to be commonplace as the gangster film genre was born. Many silent stars like Gary Cooper and Ronald Colman, with their well modulated voices, survived the transition and flourished. Others, like the previously popular John Gilbert, just disappeared from the scene.

Most cinemas offered a full programme of feature film, a second film and a cartoon. It was the advent of the talkies that unseated Felix the Cat from being the most popular cartoon character. Not only did he appear on film but his image was endorsed on a wide range of gift merchandise. Unfortunately, his creators were slow to react to the threat of the talkies and the genius of Walt Disney. As soon as Mickey Mouse arrived on the scene in 1928, his popularity overwhelmed the silent cat. The mouse's gentle character struck a chord with the public. The animation produced was superb and in Walt Disney the second genius of the screen had arrived to join Chaplin.

By now, famous literary figures were flocking to Hollywood to fuel the insatiable appetite for dialogue. The movie moguls, still unsure of what they had unleashed, continued to refer to them as 'writing the titles'. The studio bosses' interest was money rather than uplifting scripts. No matter, the public had been won over. Across London, outside cinemas the queues lengthened. Amazing entertainment was there for everyone. Quite literally, all-talking, singing and dancing.

Pola Negri.

6

Music Go Round

'Music is what feelings sound like.'
(Author unknown)

London has always echoed to the sound of street performers. Now in the post-war era they tended to be ex-servicemen, medals proudly displayed, shuffling along the kerbs of the West End, relying on the generosity of passers-by. Busking, rather than dodging bullets, hoping to scrape a living. They had been promised 'a land for heroes', but, due to physical or mental injury, they were unable to find work and were reduced to busking for a few coppers. London and the world changes, but the poor remain always. These old soldiers wear shiny suits and threadbare overcoats. They play mainly military marches with a sprinkling of popular tunes. They occasionally attempt a jazz number, but they are not alone in really failing to transmit the raw, rough edge that only black musicians seem capable of.

The Jazz Age

The twenties is often referred to as 'The Jazz Age' and yet in Britain this new and exciting art form had limited impact and was slow to develop. It was difficult to buy American records in London, and British bands offering cover versions tended to be stilted and lightweight. Something in the British character, an emotional block, held the players back. It was jazz by numbers, neutered, emasculated. The word jazz, or 'jass', was reputed to mean something so vile and obscene that English ladies coloured with embarrassment at the thought.

This evocative shot by German photographer Yva really captured the essence of the Jazz Age.

This was underlined by jazz being essentially Negro music. This tended to excite or alarm the girls, whilst British men were not sure what to make of it all. Another drawback was that jazz numbers tended to be difficult to dance to unless you lost all restraint and that really wouldn't do. A Cambridge University undergraduate, Spike Hughes, helped change perceptions with his weekly contributions in *Melody Maker*. Slowly the upper crust, led by the Prince of Wales, gave jazz their blessing. Pale-faced Londoners tried to lose their inhibitions as they jigged clumsily to rhythms that Aldous Huxley described as 'music more barbarous than any folk art for hundreds of years'. He was not alone; a critic writing in 1927 declared tetchily, 'Brows are being worn low this season.'

Jazz was also associated with an explosion of jazzy consumer goods.

Leslie Hutchinson (Hutch), born in Grenada, acquired all the trappings and affectations of an English gentleman. He was a huge cabaret star during the twenties, seen here serenading an exclusive group of diners at The Carlton in 1929.

Design conventions were cast aside as fabrics, fittings and ceramics followed the irreverent trend. The Design and Industry Association lamented that graphic design had descended into 'Negroid chaos and jazz!' Black Americans started to arrive in London after the war to replace German band members. Britain was a land of prejudice. Class snobbery was rife and most foreigners were viewed with great suspicion. 'One Englishman was worth a dozen foreign jonnies' was often quoted (and, dangerously, sometimes believed). Because there were so few blacks they were no more discriminated against than, say, a Spaniard or an Italian. At best, they could expect to be patronised.

Hutch – a smooth operator

One black man who broke the mould by effecting a manner more English than the established 'nobs' was Leslie Hutchinson, known as 'Hutch'. He was not American, but West Indian, having being born and raised in Grenada. He had, however, spent time in the States where he perfected his piano technique. He acquired the requisite pronunciation and bearing together with the determination necessary to be accepted and embraced by society. He was good-looking and elegant. He bought his suits in Savile Row and his shirts in Jermyn Street. His manner was easy and polite. He offered no threat. Along with Paul Robeson, Layton and Johnstone and other 'acceptable' black entertainers, Hutch was welcomed into the melting pot of London's high society. Royalty, aristocrats, hugely wealthy businessmen, plus sundry arty types and entertainers all sought the limelight. By 1927 Hutch was making records as well as appearing in London's most fashionable nightspots. It was Jessie Matthews who encouraged him to sing rather than just play the piano. In 1928 he signed a deal with HMV to sing songs from Noel Coward's *This Year of Grace* which were never released. The following year he moved on to Parlophone with whom he released over twenty recordings before the end of the decade including 'Button up Your Overcoat', 'Ain't Misbehavin'' and 'What is This Thing Called Love'. Whether riding in Rotten Row, hunting with the Quorn or being chauffeur-driven in his Rolls-Royce, Hutch epitomised the society that he had skilfully infiltrated. He flourished for years with his cut-glass accent and superb expertise at the piano. He bedded royalty, stars and chorus girls until a sad decline in his latter years. His list of conquests included Princess Marina of Greece, Edwina Mountbatten and Tallulah Bankhead.

Sydney Bechet

Another brilliant black performer failed miserably in his attempt to bridge the social and racial divide. Sidney Bechet could make the clarinet and saxophone sing, but he had little charm or sophistication. He was deported from Britain on attempted rape charges in 1922. He was photographed on his arrest by the Metropolitan Police wearing a smart cream homburg and a glum, somewhat insolent look. His unpredictable temperament periodically compromised his amazing career. He also ran up against the law in Paris, when he was jailed following a shoot-out in which a passer-by was injured. His music with its rhythmic drum beat and improvisations appeared to some more akin to Africa than urban America, dangerous but exciting.

Opinion was still divided when Anna Pavlova decreed that jazz dancing 'was disgusting' and she didn't think much of the music either. Was jazz and all it stood for an offer to embrace an exciting new modern life, or a fall into total moral breakdown and decadence? The jury was still out. Whilst generally the smart set took to the jazz scene, most Londoners were more comfortable with the type of music played by American bandleader Paul Whiteman. He thought the appeal of improvised jazz would be short lived. He insisted that his players read music and keep to the score. He influenced British bandleaders like Jack Payne and Jack Hylton, who were already well established by the mid twenties. Hylton's band had recorded reasonable versions of classics like 'Lady be Good' and 'Fascinating Rhythm'. Hylton went on to be a very successful impresario. He showed his business nous early on by creating and overseeing several bands, playing in a variety of different locations. He was also the first British bandleader to create a complete show rather than just play music. Soloists were expected to provide comic interludes and slapstick fun. A favourite was the trombonist pretending to be sick into his instrument, whilst another soloist would kick Hylton in the rear as he turned to conduct the orchestra.

81

The big guns – Porter, Gerschwin and Berlin

Strangely, jazz in Britain became as much associated with the Jewish community as with black Americans. This was partly because of three giants: Cole Porter, George Gershwin and Irving Berlin. Of the three, Porter was the only Christian. Gershwin's 'Rhapsody in Blue' swept across the Atlantic as if propelled by a force-ten storm. Like Hutch, Gershwin had collected a royal admirer in Prince George, later to be Duke of Kent. Berlin was already known in Britain for the wonderful 'What'll I Do' and, of course, 'Blue Skies'. In the thirties, the hits kept on coming, culminating in 'God Bless America' in 1938. It was 1929 when London welcomed Cole Porter with his music for C. B. Cochran's 'Wake up and Dream!', which included the daring 'Let's Do It' and the heart-wrenching 'What is This Thing Called Love?' Whilse these quite brilliant composers set feet tapping, and the music critic for *New York World* famously stated that 'Rhapsody in Blue' had 'made an honest woman out of jazz', the back-up for the industry was also largely Jewish. They acted as musicians, managers, publishers, producers and pluggers. It wasn't just the style of music that was changing, but promotion and distribution.

Classical music and ballet – high culture in the big smoke

'Serious' British composers now incorporated subtle jazz themes into their work. William Walton was overwhelmed by the power and possibilities of the music. He was particularly fond of the blues singer Florence Mills, who had been influenced by the traditions of African music. She was the first black female superstar. Slim, coffee coloured and attractive, she was known as 'the little blackbird'. Evelyn Waugh records visiting her dressing-room after attending the hit review *Blackbirds* only nine months before she tragically died of pelvic tuberculosis. Her funeral in Harlem drew crowds of well over a hundred thousand. There were traces of jazz in Walton's *Viola Concerto* of 1929. His friend Constant Lambert's works showed a profound jazz influence. His 1929 composition *Rio Grande* had an under-lying beat of the Charleston. Whilst studying under Vaughan Williams,

Florence Mills was the first black female superstar, seen here in a routine from the revue *Blackbirds*, staged at the London Pavilion in 1926.

the illustrator Edmund Dulac introduced Lambert to Sergei Diaghilev (of Ballet Russes fame), who commissioned him to write an update of *Romeo and Juliet*, which was first performed in Monte Carlo in 1926. Diaghilev had a massive influence, not only on the British ballet scene, but also on theatrical design. Although a giant in the artistic sense, he also understood the potential of London's affluent population for popularising ballet. He even arranged for his dancers to perform on variety bills. In 1921, he presented *The Sleeping Beauty* at the Alhambra Theatre in Leicester Square. It was a huge commercial success, despite Tchaikovsky's music being reworked and given a modern twist by Stravinsky. The sets were lavish and the costumes alone cost over £20,000. Ballet had caught the public's imagination. Londoners indulged in a bit of culture and, for a time, the Trocadero replaced its after dinner cabaret with performances of *Coppelia*.

British contemporary composers still paid lip service to Sir Edward Elgar, although in truth he was thought to represent a bygone age. By his own admission he had 'gone off the boil'. He was to conduct one final memorable performance and recording of his *Violin Concerto*. The soloist was a young prodigy, Yehudi Menuhin, who in 1929, as a twelve-year-old, had amazed his London audience with a vintage performance of Brahms' *Violin Concerto* at the Royal Albert Hall.

Birth of the Proms

London was well served with classical concerts. Impresario Robert Newman had hit on the idea of opening up the world of 'serious' music to a wider audience by organising a series of promenade concerts back in 1895. By the 1920s, these performances had become known as the Henry Wood Promenade Concerts after the conductor and organist. Wood had conducted that very first concert and had succeeded in expanding the repertoire to include works by challenging contemporary composers rather than a diet of old favourites. The series of annual concerts was held at the Queen's Hall, Langham Place, next to the BBC's new headquarters. It was in 1927 that the BBC took over the running of the concerts. The players were billed as 'Sir Henry Wood and his Symphony Orchestra' until the formation of the BBC Symphony

Orchestra in 1930. The concept of the Proms was unique at the time and the tradition carries on today with concerts relayed around the world from the Royal Albert Hall.

A night at the opera

Celebrity and stardom were normally reserved for film stars, sportsmen and popular singers, but opera was not about to be outdone. Although the leading tenor Enrico Caruso died in 1921, his recordings remained to keep his memory alive. It was, however, the Australian prima donna, Dame Nellie Melba, who continued to draw the crowds. Although nearing the end of her career, seats to see her at Covent Garden were always at a premium. She had her own dressing-room at the Opera House to which only she had the key. She had a haughty air to match her incredible voice, once stating, 'There are many duchesses, but only one Melba!' She mixed increasingly only with the titled, rich and famous. She found London drab and shabby after the war, being horrified at seeing brown tweed suits in the stalls rather than couture gowns and tiaras. She cultivated her diva status but her voice, body and will to remain supreme ahead of new emerging talent were weakening. She made her farewell performance at Covent Garden in 1926. Being a huge patriot, she had three Australian singers perform with her the roles she had made her own earlier in her career. In many respects, Nellie Melba created the template for the demanding diva. However, few who have followed can claim the enviable distinction of having a thin toast or a dessert, still popular today, being named after them!

Making sweet music

Although the sales of gramophones were soaring, it was still sheet music that generated huge profits. Printing costs were low even for small runs, whilst songs selling many thousands cost the publishers next to nothing to commission. Home entertainment was still very popular despite the growth of the wireless. Many houses had pianos in their parlour or living-room and the demand for new sheet music seemed endless. Sales of patriotic songs like 'Pack up Your Troubles' had soared during the war. Marketing was becoming more sophisticated and a photograph of a leading singer or film star would help sales significantly. In fact radio, initially seen as a threat, helped boost sales further as amateur performers sought to emulate the professionals. There were hundreds of stores across London selling sheet music alongside an array of instruments. This was the era of participation rather than just passive listening. Most pubs had a piano and singsongs in the bar were popular and helped bring the customers in. Cockney songs with rhyming slang and standards like 'I'm Forever Blowing Bubbles' and 'My Old Dutch' could be heard most nights. Film musicals were particularly popular and there was a surge in the sale of instruments, with most neighbourhoods having their own local bands. Dance halls sprang up all over London.

The comedy song

Music helps define a generation and whilst the British experienced some difficulty with the raw honesty of black American blues and jazz, they found a comfort zone in songs with lyrics that today we consider just silly. At a time when showing genuine emotion was considered to be rather poor form, they embraced comedy songs. Looking at film shot at night-clubs during the twenties, the impression is of forced jollity, rather than sophistication. The men, hair slicked back, dapper in tails, rather than masculine. The ladies, either languid or embarrassingly unco-ordinated. No smooching or signs of passion. Maybe that came later in the evening? Lyrics featuring foreign or regional accents or perhaps stammering were considered hilarious. 'Yes, We Have No Bananas', 'Horsey Hold Your Tail Up' and 'Where Do Flies Go To in the Winter Time?' had Londoners rushing to buy the sheet music. The British stiff upper lip was underscored by the speech patterns of the upper crust and copied by the emerging middle class. Listen to recordings made in the twenties and we are struck by their clipped, staccato accents, seemingly devoid of emotion no matter what they are discussing. Play a tune like 'I Lift up my Finger and I say Tweet, Tweet' and the good folk of

Jack Buchanan, a huge musical star of the twenties, who was seen as the archetypal languid Englishman was, in fact, Scottish.

London were transformed into gyrating dervishes, as if powered by some outside force.

A star who epitomised a distinctly English manner was, in fact, Scottish by birth. Jack Buchanan was handsome, tall and elegant. He sang and danced in a languid manner, which found much favour with the public. The song that he made his own was 'And Her Mother Came Too' from the revue *A–Z* in 1921. Evelyn Waugh judged him to be only 'fairly good' when seeing Buchanan appearing in the musical comedy *Boodle* at the Empire Theatre in 1925. He was also starring in a succession of films including *Bulldog Drummond's Third Round*. Jack Buchanan was instrumental in the portrayal of the stereotypical upper-crust Englishman, to be subsequently copied and developed by a long line of English actors.

Ivor Novello

'And Her Mother Came Too' was the work of David Ivor Novello. He had already written the classic patriotic song 'Keep the Home Fires Burning' in 1919 and by the 1930s the full flow of Novello's talent had been unleashed on an adoring British public. As a young man he was described as beautiful. Like many in the profession he was a homosexual, which was risky and liable to prosecution at the time. Lesbians were viewed rather more tolerantly by the public, underlined by the fact that Norah Blaney and Gwen Farrar were allowed to appear in the Royal Command Performance of 1921. This was the first of a regular annual show produced for the King and Queen Mary, in aid of the Entertainment Artistes' Benevolent Fund. Norah Blaney and Gwen Farrar first sang together entertaining the troops during the war. Norah had a pleasing, light soprano voice and was rather glamorous. Over the years she recorded 'Second-Hand Rose' and 'The Song is Ended but the Melody Lingers On'. Her version of 'Oh, Mr Porter' is sung in a cockney accent and her act with Gwen contained comedy as well as singing. In fact, Gwen Farrar was a competent cellist and part of their act involved her dragging the instrument behind her before tossing it over her shoulder. She had a deep contralto voice which blended very well with her partner.

The daughter of a baronet, Farrar was later to be linked romantically with Tallulah Bankhead.

The Command Performance gave Londoners a chance to gawp at the stars and royalty arriving for the show, a custom that is still going strong today. 1922 saw the arrival of the American Trix sisters (Helen and Josephine), who later in 1928 recorded a moving rendition of 'Glad Rag Doll'. In 1923 the show switched from the Hippodrome to the Coliseum Theatre and featured an American Loie Fuller and her marimba band. By 1925 another new home was found when the contralto Ethel Hook appeared at the Alhambra in Leicester Square. Ethel was the sister of the better known Clara Butt.

Music music everywhere

As the economic situation worsened towards the end of the decade, it fell to British composer Vivian Ellis to 'Spread a Little Happiness' with his popular number with lyrics by Clifford Grey.

> *'Even when the darkest clouds are in the sky*
> *You musn't sigh, and you musn't cry*
> *Spread a little happiness as you go by.'*

The twenties laid the foundations for the explosion of popular music to come. For the first time composers and songwriters were able to make big money. The appetite for music across a broad church was insatiable. Songwriters were promoted as personalities, rather than just performers or bandleaders. A golden age was dawning with talent like Gershwin, Irving Berlin and Cole Porter, which, arguably, has never been surpassed.

Whilst the design and manufacture of gramophones was improving, playing the music wasn't entirely passive. Automatic record changers were introduced in 1928 but you still needed to wind the machine up and regularly change the needles; a thin variety being best for soft romantic melodies, whilst a thicker type was recommended for belting out a loud number. There was music everywhere, in restaurants, theatres, cinemas where the sound of the mighty Wurlitzer soared to the rafters. The bandstands in London's parks continued to be major attractions drawing hundreds of listeners who sat on slatted chairs as they enjoyed the music of military bands on balmy summer afternoons.

As the twenties drew to a close, popular music was feeling its way towards the era of the big band sound. Music, like life, moves on but it endures far longer. Still now, we remember so much from the 1920s. Songs that we now call standards. Tunes come and go and many are consigned to the ether. But the truly great melodies linger on.

7

You Were Wonderful, Darling!

*'Show me a great actor and I'll show you a lousy husband
Show me a great actress and you've seen the devil.'*

(W. C. Fields)

Going to the theatre tended to be a rather formal occasion in the 1920s. Most continued to wear evening dress, and the excursion usually involved having a good supper either before or after the show. Perhaps this was the reason it was reckoned that only about seven per cent of the population ever went to the theatre. Another example of leisure time being segregated by class.

Music hall moments

A visit to the music hall had been a staple of working-class entertainment for a long while. And though still popular, it was under siege from a wave of new forms of entertainment. The cinema was a massive competitor for a good night out and the craze for dancing was an added magnet for the young. Even spending evenings at home had been made ever more attractive by listening to the wireless or playing the latest hits on the gramophone. Suddenly, going to the music hall had lost its lustre, at least for most of the young.

Yet, the music hall retained much of its raw appeal. It could be rough and noisy. An act 'getting the bird' was half the attraction. The audience didn't take long to start booing and cat-calling if they sensed any weakness in a performance. At least legislation, brought in forbidding eating or drinking in the auditorium, ensured no rotten fruit could be lobbed at the unfortunate act. Music hall had its roots in entertainment performed in the back room of taverns. By 1870 it had graduated to about thirty purpose-built theatres in London and the emergence of stars who toured the country. The bill was usually made up of a variety of acts, including dancers, magicians, acrobats, comedy and a star singer. It was a uniquely British form of entertainment, perhaps best compared to American vaudeville.

I can remember going to the Metropolitan in Edgware Road just after the end of the Second World War. Music hall was really in its death throes, but to a young boy it retained a huge sense of excitement. Maybe the seats were threadbare and the boxes overlooking the stage had peeling paintwork, but I didn't care. The pit orchestra, I remember, played as if in a trance. Too many nights performing to half-full houses. Once the curtain went up I was lost in what I thought was a magical experience. The audience joined in the choruses to well-known songs. They heckled a warm-up act and my mother tutted at what were doubtless some unsuitable jokes from a loud-suited comedian (although I don't think it was Max Miller). I can now imagine what excitement a show produced twenty years previously must have created. Londoners out to enjoy themselves. Inhibitions cast to the wind, a sort of theatrical knees-up!

The twenties music hall produced its own superstars. My mother told me she had been taken to see Marie Lloyd at Collins Music Hall in Islington. She was made to promise not to tell her father as Lloyd was considered to be extremely risqué. Doubtless, today we would consider her material absolutely harmless. She really relied on innuendo rather than coarseness, with numbers like 'Oh, Mr Porter' and 'My Old Man Said Follow the Van'. Although Marie worked in the States and France, she was never happier than when she was in London. She didn't even relish working in the provinces. It was, perhaps, symptomatic of the gradual decline of the music hall that she died in 1922 and another legend, Vesta Tilley, had retired two years previously. A hugely popular male impersonator, Vesta was the highest paid performer, having popularised songs like 'Burlington Bertie' and 'Following in Father's Footsteps'. She did what many an actress craved for, by marrying a real toff, Sir Walter de Frece, and going off to live in Monte Carlo.

Many stars of the future made their first appearances treading the music hall boards. Flanagan and Allen started their long and hugely successful partnership in 1924. Gracie Fields spent years touring before arriving in London in the early twenties. Within a few years, she had made such an impression that she was selected to appear in the Royal Variety Performance. George Formby and the 'Cheeky Chappie', Max Miller, were also making their way and gaining experience, which would open up a world outside the music hall. Not everyone could or wanted to. Harry Champion had first appeared back in 1888. He combined a comedy act with songs, many of which he made famous. Somehow, though, 'Boiled Beef and Carrots', 'Any Old Iron' and 'I'm Henry the Eighth, I Am' cemented him into an area of showbusiness that was already considered 'old hat'. There were venues that continued to thrive, including the Hackney Empire, which is still going strong today. Marie Lloyd lived very close to the theatre, which featured at various times Charlie Chaplin and, supposedly, Laurel and Hardy (although there is some debate about this). The Finsbury Park Empire seated over 2,000 and has a unique claim to fame. In September 1921, the audience witnessed the first sawing in half of a woman on stage. The stunt was performed by P. T. Selbit. It caused a sensation. Ladies covered their eyes and swooned. Lurid reviews told of 'this hair-raising spectacle'. Selbit was no slouch when it came to publicity, organising buckets of red dye to be washed down the drains, witnessed with horror by startled passers-by. The act was upstaged later that year by Horace Goldin. He managed to saw his attractive assistant in half whilst her head and feet protruded from the box. This time ladies fainted. This was new and thrilling and, for a time, the public flocked back.

Leslie Sarony

Leslie Sarony was a true all rounder; his roots lay in the music hall and this gave him the ability to thrive in a variety of areas. Born in 1897, he started as a dancer and vocalist in a juvenile act 'Park's Eton Boys'. He graduated to be the principal dancer in the 1928 production of *Show Boat* with Paul Robeson. The following year, he was singing with Sam Brown and Jack Hylton's orchestra in a recording of 'On Her Doorstep Last Night!' He made several other recordings with the Hylton Band and by now he was also composing popular songs, including the rather dire 'I Lift up my Finger and I say Tweet, Tweet'. He eventually contributed to over 150 recordings, twice selling over one million copies.

Gracie Fields

The migration from music hall to cabaret and theatre was to become commonplace. It was not a trend that many in the 'legitimate theatre' welcomed, as Gracie Fields was to find out. It was Sir Gerald du Maurier – actor and theatre impresario – who offered Gracie her first straight part in the West End. The play *S.O.S.* was staged at the St James Theatre in King Street. The rest of the cast were horrified at a mere music hall performer being forced on their company. As dedicated professionals they took themselves very seriously. They cold-shouldered Gracie at rehearsals, completely ignoring her. The vivacious Lancashire lass wasn't prepared to stand for the silent treatment for too long. After a couple of days, her patience exhausted, she walked into rehearsals doing cartwheels all round the room. 'Right', she said, 'can any of you buggers do that?' The ice was broken and her infectious personality won them over. They probably guessed they were looking at a future star.

Cochran, Coward and Charlot – the age of the revue

Although the 'luvvies' obviously took themselves very seriously, theatre in the twenties revolved to a large extent around comedy, musicals and revues. However, it was a period that saw a great creative explosion. Although there was a massive American influence, two British figures were at the heart of London's theatrical boom. The impresario and stage manager, Charles B. Cochran, and the young, multi-talented Noel Coward. Yet it was Cochran's great competitor, André Charlot, who collaborated with Coward in the 1923 production of *London Calling*, featuring Gertrude Lawrence singing one of Coward's first hits 'Parisian Pierrot'. The show ran for over 300 performances at the Duke of York's Theatre in St Martin's Lane. In 1925, Cochran and Coward presented the revue *On With the Dance*. The show is remembered mainly for the song 'Poor Little Rich Girl' sung by the

Charles B. Cochran, a true giant of the London stage. The producer of hugely successful musical revues, he also had an eye for emerging talent including Gertrude Lawrence and Jessie Matthews. He also collaborated with Noel Coward in the production of many of his most successful shows.

Noel Coward enjoyed one of his most productive periods during the twenties. He acted, sang and produced shows, but it was as a playwright and composer that he is mostly remembered.

French actress Alice Delysia to Hermione Baddeley. Delysia was a particular favourite of Cochran and had been under contract to him for years. The song, whilst seemingly light-hearted, took a dig at the 'Bright Young Things' and included in the lyrics the following warning:

'*In lives of leisure, the craze for pleasure steadily grows.*
Cocktails and laughter, but what comes after? Nobody knows.'

Whilst Charlot had been a pioneer in producing revues, it was Cochran who developed them to professional perfection. Known as 'Cocky' or merely 'Mr Cochran', his influence over London's theatre was immense. Even his famous chorus girls were known as 'Mr Cochran's Young Ladies'. He was lucky that his early association with Coward coincided with one of the writer's most productive phases. Coward didn't just confine himself to revues, but he was also was an actor and playwright as well as being very active in London's social scene. Coward's work was usually controversial and mildly shocking. His early play, *The Vortex*, dealt with nymphomania, drugs and a whiff of homosexuality. The following year, 1925, saw the production of *Fallen Angels* at the Globe Theatre, starring (an angel who had regularly fallen) Tallulah Bankhead. The shows came at a bewildering speed. *Hay Fever* and *On With the Dance* came out the same year and in 1927 *One Dam' Thing After Another* caused more than a few raised eyebrows. *This Year of Grace* opened in 1928 at the London Pavilion and had two massive hits, 'A Room With a View' and 'Dance Little Lady, Dance!'. The following year Cochran produced *Bittersweet*, billed as an operetta, in which Coward is said to have been influenced by the works of Gilbert and Sullivan. Although not as controversial as much of his work, the show was a great success and featured one of Coward's best-loved songs, 'I'll See You Again'.

Oliver Messel

Like many entrepreneurs, Cochran was a great spotter of talent. The young stage designer Oliver Messel had worked on creating masks for a 1925 production of Diaghilev's *Zephyr et Flore*. His potential was

An evening at the theatre.

obvious and they worked together for the first time on *This Year of Grace*. Messel brought a new and original approach to stage design. Described as a master of theatrical illusion, he had the ability to transform seemingly run of the mill material into things of stunning, visual beauty. His stage settings, whilst stylised, were elegant and memorable, providing the finishing touches to subsequent Cochran revues.

Theatre tickets in the West End were no longer cheap, with prices for the stalls and dress circle normally costing about 12/6, whilst the pit was available at 3/6. As drink was no longer available in the auditorium, strategically placed bars were much in demand during intervals. Trays of tea were served for the more sober minded. Whilst the London theatre of the twenties has been dismissed by some as escapist and trivial, it was still possible to get your fill of Shakespeare and 'serious' highbrow fare such as Chekhov's *The Seagull* and *Uncle Vanya* or Ibsen's *Hedda Gabler* and the *Wild Duck* – if that was what floated your boat. George Bernard Shaw was in full flow with two of his more successful plays, *Saint Joan* and *Heartbreak House*, which attracted Sybil Thorndyke and Edith Evans to the leading roles. A rather beautiful John Gielgud, who had understudied Noel Coward in *The Vortex*, appeared in *The Insect Play* by Karel and Josef Capek. He was the 'poet butterfly', sporting white flannels and wings. By 1929, he was being acclaimed in the first of two seasons he spent at the Old Vic theatre.

Rather like the poets, playwrights took some time to confront the horrors of the Great War. R. C. Sherriff's *Journey's End* made an enormous impact. It was acclaimed by American Alex Woollcott as 'the finest work yet wrought by an Englishman out of his war experiences'. Sherriff insisted it was not a pacifist play, but it certainly underlined the futility of war. Colin Clive took the lead role of a commanding officer who is cracking under the strain. An unknown Laurence Olivier had taken the part in a pre-production run, but was unable to appear in the West End production as he had subsequently landed the lead in *Beau Geste*.

It's showtime – the musical has arrived

1925 saw the arrival of the first spectacular American musical *Rose Marie*, starring Edith Day. Its staging at Theatre Royal, Drury Lane, must have been particularly welcome as there had been a series of disastrous shows since its reconstruction in 1922. The show ran for almost 600 performances. The public's appetite for musicals was insatiable. They were not disappointed. There were memorable productions of *The Student Prince*, *The Desert Sons* and in 1923 *Show Boat*. This musical had a far more serious theme than the usual light-hearted, escapist shows. It dared to bring underlying racism to the stage. Oscar Hammerstein said he wept whenever he heard his own lyrics from the show. With music by Jerome Kern, it had memorable songs, including 'Ole Man River' and 'Can't Help Lovin' Dat Man of Mine'. Based on the book by Edna Ferber, it was important in being the first time white and black performers held the stage together as equals.

An earlier Kern and Hammerstein musical *Sunny* had a successful run at The Hippodrome, featuring British stars Jack Buchanan and Binnie Hale.

Jessie Matthews

Perhaps the greatest emerging British star was Jessie Matthews, whose real life experiences were often more outlandish than the roles she performed. She was born into a huge family in Soho. Her father was a street trader, who set off each morning in his horse-drawn cart. She recalls the smell and warmth of the horse filling her shared bedroom from the stable below. She made her debut at the Metropolitan in Edgware Road in 1919. She was a chorus girl in a Charlot revue and understudied Gertrude Lawrence when it transferred to New York. She was waif-like but sexy, with dark brown eyes and a toothy grin. Having won acclaim in the States, she was one of the first to perform Coward's 'A Room With a View', and in 1928 Cole Porter's 'Let's Do It, Let's Fall in Love'. She stayed with various Charlot revues until taking the lead in *One Dam' Thing After Another* in 1927. She teamed up with Noel Coward again the following year with Sonnie Hale in *This Year of Grace*. As far as Sonnie Hale was concerned, 'teamed up' took on rather more significance. The two were cited in a sensational divorce case brought by Sonnie's wife, 'Boo' Laye. While she was in Hollywood making the film *One Heavenly Night*, her husband and Britain's sex symbol Jessie Matthews were enjoying a few of their own. The scandal, with its lurid court details, stopped Jessie's career for a time. She was dubbed an immoral husband-snatcher. Luckily for her, the presence she showed on stage transferred perfectly to film and she became for a time Britain's major international star.

Fred Astaire

Another American phenomenon hit Britain's shores in the shape of Adele and Fred Astaire. Encouraged by Noel Coward and the impresario Sir Alfred Butt, they premiered in *Stop Flirting* with music by Gershwin, including 'I'll Build a Stairway to the Stars'. The show and the Astaires were given rave reviews. The show was attended by both the King and the Prince of Wales, and soon the brother and sister combination were enjoying a social whirl of fashionable restaurants and country house weekends. They returned in 1926 to the Empire, Leicester Square, with *Lady Be Good*. This was another smash hit with music and lyrics by George and Ira Gershwin, including the standard 'Fascinating Rhythm'. Their last appearance in London was to star in *Funny Face*, featuring ''S Wonderful', which became an instant hit. Adele obviously took to the good life, retiring after marrying Lord Charles Cavendish and lived happily ever after. Well, not quite! They divorced later, but Lady Cavendish does have a nice ring to it.

The theatre in all its forms was central to Londoners' constant zest for entertainment. A succession of musicals created memorable tunes and lyrics, which we still love today. This is largely due to the twenties being the first era where the music of the theatre and the dance band was secured for future generations in the recording studio. It truthfully represents the age of the flappers – and all that jazz!

101

8

The Cat's Whiskers

'Radio – because some pictures need a thousand words.'

(Author unknown)

The British Broadcasting Company was created by a consortium of radio manufacturers. They looked enviously across the Atlantic where, by 1922, $60 million worth of radio sets had already been sold. They may well have foreseen an industry financed by advertising, and yet they should have known this was not the British way. Broadcasting in Britain would shun commercialism and the profit motive.

Britain's tentative entry into the world of the wireless had been gloriously amateurish. For almost three years the Marconi Company had been broadcasting to a smattering of enthusiastic listeners. In 1921 they had even managed to get the redoubtable Dame Nellie Melba to sing a series of patriotic songs. Her broadcast had been subsidised by Lord Northcliffe, who sensed the explosion of radio audiences would significantly reduce the circulation of his papers. Being a shrewd businessman, he took the precaution of renting a radio station in Holland – a form of each-way bet. Dame Nellie bellowed out her renditions so loudly that some joked she had no need for the large trumpet-like microphone.

John Reith – the man at the Beeb

People belonging to the Radio Society of Great Britain were able to listen to Station 2MT, which had a licence to broadcast gramophone selections and vocal content. The shows were frequently shambolic.

John Reith, huge in stature and reputation, oversaw the creation of the BBC and its development into a national institution.

Valuable time was being wasted, a more professional approach was essential. Early in 1922 a tall, angular figure strode down Kingsway to attend an interview for the post of General Manager of the British Broadcasting Company. John Reith cut an austere, yet imposing figure. He stood six feet six inches tall and his left cheek was badly scarred from a sniper's bullet he had received in the war. Reith was the son of a Scottish Free Church minister and his strict upbringing continued to influence his thoughts and decisions throughout his life. It is easy to understand why he didn't feel particularly well equipped for the job advertised. After being injured and whilst still a serving officer, he had been sent to the States to work at the Remington Arms Company. He was in charge of a team of inspectors checking rifles which were due to be consigned to the battlefields of Europe. He was one of the first Englishmen who had been wounded in action to visit America, and this appeared to open doors for him to meet influential financial figures, including J. D. Rockefeller. These contacts in turn helped introduce him to leading politicians on his return to Britain, including British statesman Austen Chamberlain and Prime Minister David Lloyd George. Powerful connections doubtless helped his application and he was duly appointed General Manager of the British Broadcasting Company, at a healthy annual salary of £1,750 per year.

Reith set about forming a team to take on the exciting challenge of bringing programmes to a far wider audience. His key appointment was Captain Peter Eckersley as Chief Executive. Eckersley, a former wireless equipment officer, had been a leading light in 2MT. He had latterly taken to acting as an unofficial compère and record presenter. He was largely responsible for introducing the true art of communication into British broadcasting. Within a year of Reith's and Eckersley's appointments, over half a million licences had been purchased. Everyone was talking about the new miracle of the wireless. By 1924, the take up had doubled, and in 1927 almost 3 million homes had a radio. This was a revolution in modern technology, as far-reaching as the Internet has been today.

Olive Sturgess and John Huntingdon perform a duet during an early broadcast from BBC Marconi House in 1922.

Early years at the BBC

It was in November 1922 that the British Broadcasting Company transmitted its first programme from Savoy Hill in London. Its call sign was '2LO calling'. The programme was a mixture of news, weather and, importantly, the first coverage of election results. Initially, there were regional stations, each with their own call signs. The installation of a high-powered transmitter at Daventry allowed more ambitious programming to be developed. Christopher Stone became a household name as one of Britain's first disc jockeys, albeit a very dry one who only played classical music. The writer, Compton Mackenzie, was also one of the first to spin the turntable. A very limited diet of popular music was provided by the coloured American double act, Layton and Johnstone. The first radio comedy featured Helena Millais playing 'Our Lizzie' in 1922. The following year, the first comedian to feature was John Henry with his wife Blossom. 'Wireless Willie' was not far behind with his mixture of comic songs and patter. One of radio's early legends, the comedian Tommy Handley, weighed in with his shows *Disorderly Room* and in 1925 *Radio Radiance*. Today, the humour appears utterly banal but the public wanted to be taken out of the harsh realities of the times and they giggled and laughed on cue. They presumably even enjoyed a character calling himself 'Stainless Stephen'. His sole gimmick was literally to punctuate every gag he told ('A funny thing, comma, happened on my way to the studio tonight, full stop'). As all shows were broadcast live, things frequently went wrong. Unlike in the early days of television, the radio producers didn't have the potter's wheel to fall back on. Lengthy silences were sometimes interspersed with light music, where a group such as the Gershom Parkington Quintet would be on hand to fill the gap.

1923 saw the introduction of regular weather forecasts and the publication of the *Radio Times*. Newspaper proprietors had seen the wireless as a threat to their circulation figures. Initially, Reith teamed up with Gordon Selfridge, who listed programme schedules in his advertisements featured in the *Pall Mall Gazette*. In the September of 1923 the *Radio Times* was launched under the banner of 'The Official Organ of the BBC'. It came out weekly each Friday and was priced at tuppence. Initially, it was a joint venture with the publisher George Newnes, but by 1925 the BBC had taken over editorial control. The wireless had royal blessing from the outset with the news that Heals had made an outstanding cabinet for the King's own wireless in 1922. Two years later, he became the first royal to address the nation at the British Empire Exhibition from Wembley. It was also in 1924 that the Greenwich time signal (the pips) was first heard. By now the radio manufacturers were in full swing, with W. G. Pye & Co. advertising the very latest two-valve set.

Outside broadcasts

From the beginning, Reith had been keen on outside broadcasts. His efforts to cover the wedding of the Duke of York to the future Queen Mother were rebuffed by Westminster Abbey, as was coverage of the

Remembrance Day service from the Cenotaph. Not easily sidetracked, the BBC duly relayed a performance of the *Magic Flute* from Covent Garden. This was followed by the first running commentary of an outside event, when the Lord Mayor's show was broadcast. Some of the early outside broadcasts were particularly bizarre. In 1924, an attempt was made to broadcast a nightingale from deepest Surrey. The wretched bird was supposedly encouraged by the playing of a cello by a virtuoso called Beatrice Harrison. After what seemed like an eternity, a tweet was heard from the woods of Oxted, which was transmitted around the Empire.

Like the newspaper proprietors, sports promoters were very wary of coverage of their events. They were convinced that commentaries would affect their gates, whereas it actually encouraged more people to attend. By 1927, rugby matches were being broadcast with the help of a grid diagram illustrated in the *Radio Times*. Many of these early broadcasts were farcical, with George Atkinson's racing commentaries becoming legendary as he forgot the names of the runners, possibly under instructions as Reith objected to gambling. He was also averse to scandal, sex and divorce. Although Peter Eckersley had been such an important part of the early success of the BBC, he was forced to resign in 1927 after his marriage broke up and he married a divorcée.

Inform, educate, entertain

From its conception, Reith had an unshakeable belief that it was the BBC's job to educate the great British public. 'Inform, educate and entertain' became something of a mantra. Special programmes were produced for schools. As early as 1922 *Children's Hour* was introduced. The sense of the BBC being an extension of the family was underlined by the presenters of *Children's Hour* being referred to as 'uncle' or 'aunty'. In 1922, the first uncle was Arthur Burrows (Uncle Arthur). By 1926, Derek McCullock had joined the show and for generations to come was fondly known as Uncle Mac. Adults were also treated to talks on history, literature and classical music. This was all rather more Radio 4 than Radio 1! In 1927, the BBC started broadcasting the Henry Wood Promenade concerts. This coverage helped popularise the event, which had previously been in danger of folding through poor attendance. It was in 1927 that the BBC became a corporation rather than a company. Now Reith had to contend with a board of governors, instead of the directors whom he had rather overwhelmed previously. Some of the new appointees didn't meet with his approval. The feeling was mutual and he was viewed as being remote and autocratic. The BBC's new motto was 'Nation shall speak unto nation'. That sounded fine, but Reith was not about to be so liberal where his home audience was concerned. His directives to programme makers were prescriptive. Comedians could, for example, tell jokes about the Irish, but not the Welsh. Obviously, jokes relating to Scots were totally off limits. Religion was also a no-go area, and even gags about the effects of alcohol were banned. It was not long before dissenting voices were heard. Why were there no rational discussions on religion or politics? Programmes were being sanitised. There was to be no mention of murders, scandal or, heaven preserve us, sex. The very subjects that encouraged people to buy newspapers were banned or severely frowned upon. It was also noticeable that well modulated Oxford accents dominated the airwaves. This, despite the fact that Reith retained his distinctive Aberdonian accent. The initial enthusiasm that had greeted the formation of the BBC now gave way to a storm of criticism. Letters were written to the press and the BBC demanding more popular music and light entertainment. Listeners were fed up with hours of dirge and long serious plays. There was no immediate breakthrough. Indeed, a committee was set up to stipulate a correct BBC pronunciation for a huge range of words and place names. Decency, standards and fair play had to be upheld. Much emphasis continued to be directed at the children's audience. The programmes were all 'frightfully nice' in an attempt to drag youngsters, even from the most deprived backgrounds, to believe in a world that the BBC endorsed. So straight-laced and buttoned-up was the BBC's delivery that announcers, such as Stuart Hibberd, even wore dinner jackets for evening broadcasts.

Nevertheless, listening to the wireless had become a national obsession. From expensive service flats in Kensington and Mayfair to the two-up, two-down terraced houses of Battersea and Hoxton, the radio was seldom switched off. Youngsters listened in bed to crystal sets, scarcely daring to breathe for fear that the cat's whisker would fall off the crystal. Crystal sets needed no external power or battery. The energy was derived from radio waves sent from the transmitter of the radio station. Crystal sets were particularly popular with the young because they were cheap, often being supplied in kit form. If a radio programme didn't appeal there was always the gramophone to fall back on. This enabled you to play records of your own choice, rather than the serious works favoured by the BBC. Hundreds of small manufacturers started producing a huge range from the humble crystal set to sophisticated gramophones housed in custom-built mahogany cases. Early models had huge trumpets for transmitting the sound, and constant attention had to be given to winding up the mechanism to ensure the music was played at the right speed.

Other exciting developments were in their embryonic stages. There was talk of a 'seeing wireless'. In 1925, it was claimed that black and white silhouettes were being transmitted. Another Scot, John Logie Baird, was on the verge of an invention that would have a massive impact on society. In 1926, he made a presentation to the Royal Institution of Great Britain. Unfortunately for Baird, his method of scanning never managed to achieve high definition, and it was left to others to invent the cathode-ray tube and develop the modern television we take for granted today. For now though, it was the radio that was transforming the leisure time of the entire population. It was to provide a platform for the stars and household names of the future. Unlike the commercial radio of America, the BBC gradually became the cosy, welcoming 'aunty' that could be trusted with its impartial views, and it increasingly set out not just to educate, but to entertain.

9

Read all About it

'A good book on your shelf is a friend that turns its back on you and remains a friend.'

(Author unknown)

London was the centre of the publishing world. Improved education standards ensured that the twenties were a golden age for reading. A primary source for gaining knowledge or just relaxing. Newspapers, magazines, cheap thrillers, pretentious novels and some worthy classics were all devoured by a public whose appetite was hard to satisfy. Regular visits were made to public libraries, where it was possible to take out several books at a time. Boots and other retailers also had lending library sections within their stores. What then were Londoners reading?

The daily rag

Daily newspapers were read on buses or whilst strap-hanging on the Underground. There was a fierce circulation war going on in the popular press. The front pages were largely devoted to advertisements: small classifieds in the *Times* and *Telegraph*, whilst the *Mail* carried larger and more eye-catching ads. The *Daily Mail* was known for its stunts and competitions. It was locked in an arm wrestle with the *Express* for the valuable middle market. Those with left-wing tendencies had a choice between the *Daily Herald* or the *Mirror*, which had a daily circulation of over a million. The Liberals, aware of their decline in popularity, attempted to address the drift by launching their own paper, the *Westminster Gazette* in 1921. It struggled on for seven years before being absorbed into the *Daily News*, eventually reinventing itself as the *News Chronicle*. London also supported a number of evening papers, including the Evening News and Standard. Lord Beaverbrook had added the *Standard* to his stable in 1923 and, although no official circulation figures were kept, it was reckoned that the *Evening News* was selling around 300,000 copies each day. Gossip columns and beauty tips were important, as were cartoon strips, in an attempt to attract readers. Competition even extended to the racing tipsters, whose successes were splashed over the sporting sections. Sunday papers were more salacious and the *News of the World, Reynold's News* and the *Sunday Dispatch* all vied for the latest sensational scandal.

The glossies

The magazine market was also enjoying substantial growth. The *Spectator, New Statesman* and the *Nation,* who concentrated on political and world events, had relatively small circulations but an influential readership. The real expansion belonged to women's interest magazines like *Woman and Home,* whose cosy preoccupation with knitting patterns was shaken by the arrival of *Good Housekeeping* in 1922. It was an anglicised version of the American edition created by the Hearst Corporation. It was glossy and confident. It tested everyday products and those passing muster were given its seal of approval. This in turn led to additional advertising as manufacturers proudly announced their accolade. The magazine also attracted an impressive line-up of leading writers, including A. J. Cronin and Somerset Maughan. Soon competition arrived with the launch of *Homes and Gardens,* published by Condé Nast. *Vogue* was another magazine that was initially almost identical to its American counterpart, apart from its anglicised spelling. It quickly established itself as the fashion magazine against which all others were judged. It was bought mainly by women who couldn't remotely afford the sleek gowns and dresses illustrated. Each edition had a stunning front cover, many of which over the years have achieved iconic status.

Those wishing to keep up with the social scene needed to look no further than the *Tatler*. It covered all the great social events – Ascot, Henley, Wimbledon – as well as featuring endless photographs of lumpy ladies astride their hunters, or with their husbands at a point to point in deepest Leicestershire. If you had a title, a military rank above that of captain or, at the very least, a double-barrelled name, your chances of being featured were pretty good. It is striking how wonderful the line drawings for dresses and gowns appear in advertisements, whilst in contrast most of those photographed in *Tatler* look so frumpy. This image was offset by Lewis Baumer's colourful illustrations of what simply became known as the 'Baumer girls'. Rival publication the *Bystander* appealed to a similar readership before being absorbed by *Tatler* in 1940.

Whilst the ladies of the house flicked through the society and fashion magazines, their maids were drawn towards the *Red Star Weekly* or the *Red Magazine*. These featured romantic yarns, which were constantly recycled from editions published years earlier. They offered a temporary escape from their lives of drudgery. Handsome heroes and a tender kiss on the cheek was just about as shocking as it got.

The *Bystander* was a weekly magazine featuring social news and gossip. It also published short stories and articles by many of Britain's best known writers. It was a rival to *Tatler*, with which it merged in 1940.

113

Punch was already an institution by the 1920s, and although widely read, it was to the cartoons that many turned first. E. H. Shepard, Heath Robinson and Steven Spurrier were all regular contributors. Perhaps best known for his work during the period was H. M. Bateman, who was reckoned to be the highest paid cartoonist with many of his drawings being produced as prints. He was reputed to be earning about £4,000 per year by 1930. He also produced weekly drawings for the theatrical page of *Tatler*. Other popular magazines included *Nash's* and *Britannia*, both of which concentrated on home and fashion design, whilst attracting celebrated authors to contribute. There was even a *Happy Magazine*, where all the stories had a happy ending. *Pearson's Weekly* was the first magazine to introduce a crossword puzzle in 1924, followed swiftly by the *Daily Express*. In 1926, in recognition of the huge interest in popular music, the *Melody Maker* was born.

Children's comics would also prove to be a lucrative market for the publishers. *Chums* was aimed at boys, with detective and adventure yarns. A popular annual was produced for the Christmas market. There was a large selection of comics normally featuring a strip cartoon format with the storyline applicable to each picture printed underneath. The titles of the comics suggest that the editors wanted to promote light-hearted enjoyment. *Merry* and *Bright, Lot-O-Fun, Chuckles, Happy Jester,* all sought to promote an age of innocence. Tiger Tim was one of the most popular characters, but like the majority of the titles he has fallen by the wayside. *Tiny Tots*, launched in 1927, did at least last until 1959.

Fiction for all

This was also a vintage era for fiction. The author thought to most represent 'The Jazz Age' was F. Scott Fitzgerald. In 1920, aged twenty-three, he published *This Side of Paradise*. Embarrassingly, he described it as 'a novel written about flappers for philosophers'. It was thought by the young that he glamourised and justified their way of life, yet Fitzgerald was actually out to satirise this very same set. *The Beautiful and the Damned* was followed in 1925 by *The Great Gatsby*, which created a sensation on both sides of the Atlantic.

Making even greater waves in Britain was *The Green Hat* written by an Armenian living in London who had changed his name to Michael Arlen. Although public school educated and mixing in high society, he suffered from the inherent mistrust of foreigners harboured by many Britons. Despite his immaculate dress and perfect manners he never quite 'cut the mustard'. In fact, it was yellow that really let him down.

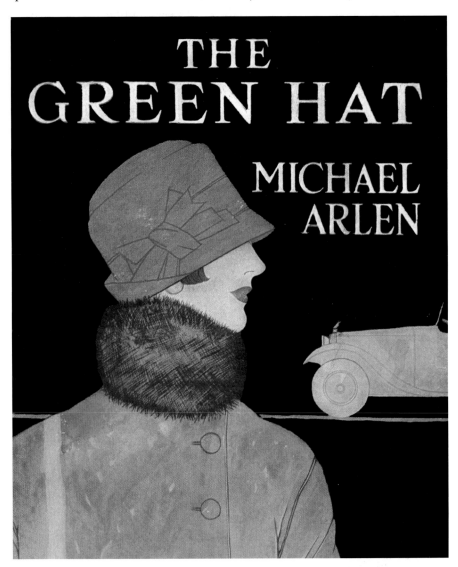

The Green Hat was a sensation when published in 1924. It blew the hat off the London social scene, leaving everyone to ponder who the leading characters were based on.

What dreadful taste he showed by driving a yellow Rolls-Royce to advertise his wealth. Fellow novelist Sydney Horler once declared that Arlen was 'the only Armenian who never tried to sell me a carpet'. No matter, Michael Arlen skewered London high society with a novel that caused shock, alarm and outrage. The standard of his writing in no way matched Fitzgerald's but the content did. Fashionable London is portrayed as sleazy, immoral and ultimately sad. Iris (the heroine, if that's what she is) has to endure her husband committing suicide on their wedding night after confessing he has syphilis. Iris continues to take a succession of lovers but it brings her no joy. She speaks of her 'soiled loneliness of desire' before driving her yellow Hispano-Suiza into a tree and killing herself. Society was now awash with rumours. A guessing game was underway. Which characters in the book matched the people that Arlen had been mixing with socially? The book made him a fortune and was produced as a play. In an inspired piece of typecasting, Tallulah Bankhead played Iris. By 1928 Hollywood had got in on the act with the film starring Greta Garbo. In the same year, Arlen bagged Countess Atalanta Mercati as his wife in the exotic surroundings of Cannes. He continued to be a prolific author but none of his subsequent works had the power to shock like *The Green Hat*.

Not everyone was fascinated by the goings-on in high society. For those looking for excitement there were plenty of tales of adventure and derring-do. Fictional heroes tended to be drawn from the officer class, like Bulldog Drummond and Berry Pleydell. The creator of Bulldog Drummond was Herman McNeile who wrote under the pen name of Sapper. This was because he started writing whilst still a serving officer in the army and was banned from using his own name. Drummond was depicted as an ex-officer with time on his hands, setting out to defeat a range of crooks, many of whom were, of course, foreigners. These right-wing heroes sought to maintain their social and racial authority in a rapidly changing world. The genre is possibly best summed up by a book written years later *Snobbery with Violence* by Marion Chesney.

The crime scene

Edgar Wallace was the most prolific writer of crime novels, completing over 150 during a long career. An ex-policeman, he was able to bring

116

a certain authenticity to his stories, which tended to be well plotted but appallingly written. Why should he have worried? He was probably the country's highest paid living author with many of his stories being made into films. He was also the co-creator of *King Kong*.

Detective stories have always been popular and the twenties threw up a number of vintage authors. Perhaps the best known was Agatha Christie, otherwise known as 'The Queen of Crime'. Her first novel, *The Mysterious Affair* (1920), featured her famous Belgian detective Hercule Poirot. He subsequently appeared in dozens of other tales and still fascinates television audiences today, as does her other great character, Miss Marple. An elderly lady solving the most heinous crimes struck a nerve with the public. A real life drama surrounded Agatha Christie when she disappeared for eleven days in 1926. She was eventually tracked down to the Old Swan Hotel in Harrogate where she had registered under a false name. She had supposedly discovered that her husband had been unfaithful to her. The less charitable attributed her disappearance to a publicity stunt as it coincided with the publication of her latest novel, *The Murder of Roger Ackroyd*. This was a very original tale in that the narrator turns out to be the murderer.

Margery Allingham and Dorothy L. Sayers were also prolific crime writers of the period whose iconic detectives were very much establishment figures. Allingham was first published as a nineteen-year-old, but it was 1929 before Albert Campion arrived on the scene. Later in life she described him (in her early tales) as 'a silly ass'. Eventually his character developed into a rather mild, but intelligent upper crust detective. Though her key character bears little resemblance to the real police, her stories were well constructed and sufficiently intricate to keep the reader's interest.

The focus on aristocratic detectives continued with Dorothy L. Sayers' best known character, Lord Peter Wimsey. He first appeared in *Whose Body?* in 1923. Sayers described him as being a cross between Fred Astaire and Bertie Wooster. He featured in over a dozen novels and short stories. She was the most literate of a generation of crime authors. Her plots were minutely researched, as was her detailed knowledge of poisons. She has undoubtedly had an influence on some of today's writers with their concentration on forensic crime.

P. G. Wodehouse

P. G. Wodehouse also concentrated on the aristocracy for many of his characters, although in his case the emphasis was on comedy. Jeeves and Wooster have come to represent for us the essence of the twenties with its snobbery, manner of speech and catchphrases. He was particularly good when conveying the exaggerated drawl and phraseology of London clubroom slang. Yet there was more to Wodehouse than parody, and his gentle debunking of the social scene with his hapless, chinless wonders and frightening harridans, ranks him as one of the great comedy writers of the twentieth century. He was also a talented lyricist, teaming up with both Jerome Kern and Cole Porter. His seemingly effortless writing style was appreciated by many of his contemporaries, including Rudyard Kipling and Evelyn Waugh.

Foreign and exotic settings for novels were also irresistible to readers. International travel was only open to the very few and when P. C. Wren's *Beau Geste* hit the bookstands in 1924 its success was pretty well assured. The mysteries of the French Foreign Legion were revealed by Wren, who had travelled extensively across North Africa. There was a fascination with all things Arabic, helped no doubt by Rudolph Valentino's performance in *The Sheik*.

War stories

With almost a decade past, a number of books appeared dealing with the Great War and life in the trenches. Perhaps it had taken time for the writers to come to terms with the horrors that each had been exposed to. In 1929 Robert Graves' *Goodbye To All That* was released, an autobiographical account of the war. In it he infers that British and Commonwealth troops executed prisoners of war. In a damning indictment he goes on to question many traditional British values. In the same year another book *Death of a Hero* by Richard Aldington heavily criticised the way the war was conducted. This was his first novel and he vividly recreates the horrors of the war in which he fought and was wounded. Despite his objections, much of the swearing and profanity in the dialogue was censored. Siegfried Sassoon was already a household name before the publishing of his *Memoirs of an Infantry Officer*. Famously, in 1917, he had decided not to return to the trenches by sending a letter explaining his reasons to his commanding officer. This was despite having been awarded the military cross for conspicuous bravery, and being described as 'Mad Jack' by his men because of his lack of concern for his own safety. The government decided it would be counter-productive to charge a war hero for treason and Sassoon was shipped off to Craiglockhart hospital in Scotland to be treated for shell-shock. Author, diplomat and politician Harold Nicholson described *Memoirs of an Infantry Officer* as 'a book of deep beauty and abiding significance'.

Despite the quality and depth of feeling conveyed by these British authors, it fell to a German, Erich Maria Remarque, to write the ultimate anti-war book with his shockingly moving *All Quiet on the Western Front*. The book touched a nerve that none of the others quite managed and caused great controversy. It didn't seem right to be sympathising with the enemy, but the narrative cut right through long-held prejudices. It was written in a cool, almost detached style, which was all the more devastating. In its first year, the book sold over a million copies. In 1930 a film was made, which has itself become a classic. Astonishingly, it was banned in France until 1962.

Of course, Graves and Sassoon were also formidable poets, but it is the works of Rupert Brooke and Wilfred Owen that we generally associate with the Great War. Perhaps their deaths at an early age projected their work into posthumous fame, but there is no doubting the poignancy of their poems. Brooke saw little active service but he died needlessly from a minor wound that was neglected. He died of blood poisoning. His work, gentler in tone than other war poets, created an intense feeling of patriotism and his poems were still being widely read in the 1920s. Wilfred Owen died tragically just one week before the end of the war. Having been gassed, he had met up with Sassoon at the hospital just outside Edinburgh. Like Sassoon, he was also awarded the military cross. Owen held Sassoon in such esteem that it has been likened to hero worship, and yet it is Owen's works that linger longer as this shocking passage from *Dulce et Decorum Est* proves:

'Gas! Gas! Quick, boys! An ecstasy of fumbling
Fitting the clumsy helmets just in time.
But someone still was yelling and stumbling
And flound'ring like a man in fire or lime
Dim through the misty panes and thick green light
As under a green sea, I saw him drowning.'

Wilfred Owen's powerful *Collected Poems* was published in 1920.

One-track minds – sex and the novel

For those trying to forget about the war, what better way than sex? There was plenty on offer, at least in its printed form, even from well-known intellectuals like Aldous Huxley. His 1923 novel *Antic Hay* threw in devil worship, nymphomania and drug taking. The subject matter may have been scandalous, but the writing was so dry and academic that it was in no way titillating. *Ulysses* by James Joyce had to be printed in Paris and hundreds of copies were confiscated by Customs. Hardly an easy read, it was considered by T. S. Elliot to demonstrate that Joyce was 'the greatest master of the English language since Milton'.

The writer with a real obsession with sex was, of course, D. H. Lawrence. He was one of the few working-class authors to flourish during the twenties. He had already had several works published before the war, but he began to gain some notoriety with his 1920 novel *Women in Love*. This was followed by other works, including *The Ladybird* and *The Plumed Serpent*. Then, in 1928, *Lady Chatterley's Lover* arrived to shock, thrill and outrage. Not only was it sexually explicit, it challenged social norms. The fact that titled ladies had been having affairs with grooms and servants for centuries was not the point – it was wrong and dangerous to write about it. Working men would be roused and get silly ideas. It had to be banned. It was, both in Britain and the States. This, of course, only increased the demand. Like the artist Augustus John, Lawrence had been helped and encouraged by Lady Ottoline Morrell. Her house, Garsington Manor, near Oxford, drew artists, writers and pseudo-intellectuals like moths to light. They all used her, some abused her and generally repaid her hospitality by being catty and wounding behind her back. Lawrence is thought to have based Hermione Roddice in *Women in Love* on Ottoline.

Nancy Cunard and the Sitwells also prided themselves on spotting and developing talent. Nancy Cunard not only helped in getting the aspiring writers' work published but there was a fair chance they would also get to share her bed. Her conquests read like a *Who's Who* of twentieth-century figures. Louis Gordon, in his biography of Nancy, explains that amongst many others, Ezra Pound, T. S. Eliot, Aldous Huxley and Wyndham Lewis all became her lovers. As did Ernest Hemingway, whose first novel *The Sun also Rises* was well reviewed, though it was *A Farewell to Arms* that won him a huge following in Britain, perhaps helped by the fact that the heroine was a British nurse caught up in a great and moving love affair. Hemingway's taut, spare style still feels refreshingly modern today.

Hemingway's novels set in Italy, and particularly Spain, appealed to a British audience hungry for tales about foreign lands. They were wary of foreigners but interested in where they came from.

Somerset Maugham fed them a feast of short stories about the South Seas and his 1922 novel *East of Suez* found particular favour. Compton MacKenzie was a prolific author completing over a hundred novels. Although he published over ten titles during the twenties, including *Gramophone Nights* in 1923, none of his work was to compare with his two best-known novels *Sinister Street* and *Carnival*, published a decade earlier. Having been in British Intelligence during the war, he ran into trouble by criticising what he termed 'scores of unemployed generals' in *Greek Memories*, a book that was subsequently withdrawn and all copies destroyed. He was fined £100 for contravening the Official Secrets Act.

A great publishing success of the 1920s was J. B. Priestley's *The Good Companions*. His publishers had been very wary because of its length, which meant that the book had to be sold for more than 7/6, which was thought to be the most the public would pay. They need not have worried as it was the publishing hit of 1928. The story follows a troupe of actors moving from town to town. The *Times* critic reported, 'The *Good Companions* is the perfect novel for the deckchair on the beach.' It was safe, reassuring and undemanding, just what the public needed.

Elizabeth Bowen and Rosamond Lehmann were both talented writers at the beginning of their careers. Lehmann's *Dusty Answer,* published in 1927, received great critical acclaim. This, despite her heroine flirting with the gay and lesbian scene at Cambridge University. Beautiful and gullible, Lehmann's private life turned out to be more dramatic than anything contained in her novels. A biography by Selina Hastings has revived interest in a writer who had fallen off the radar.

Evelyn Waugh

Evelyn Waugh was a major talent who was also just embarking on a career that now ranks him as the most brilliant observer of the British social scene. Waugh's first novel *Decline and Fall* was published by Chapman and Hall, having been turned down by Duckworth as obscene. Like many first novels, it relied to a great extent on his own experiences. He was able to capture perfectly the contemporary London social scene of the well-to-do. He wrote with a wonderful economy of words. He was the master of the short paragraph and the even shorter sentence. The book received critical acclaim, but it was his next novel that proved to be a massive, popouar success. *Vile Bodies* is surely a masterpiece. Waugh dedicated the book to his friends Bryan and Diana Guinness, the third Mitford sister, later to marry Oswald Mosley. Evelyn Waugh, describing her, said, 'her beauty ran through the room like a peal of bells'. *Vile Bodies* shines a shaft of light on the Bright Young People. It is a satire on their fast cars, fast women and the endless parties; the louche behaviour and changing moral values; of a lifestyle that cannot be sustained, an era limping to an end. It is Waugh who must have the final say, moaning about a problem suffered by all writers. Sitting at his desk at his father's house in Golders Green back in September 1927, he writes:

How I hate this household and how ill I feel in it. The whole place volleys and thunders with traffic. I can't sleep or work. I reviewed the books and have started a comic novel. Mother is at Midsomer Norton where Aunt Trissie is dying. The telephone bell is continually ringing, my father scampering up and down stairs, Gaspard barking, the

122

gardener rolling the gravel under the window and all the time the traffic. Another week of this will drive me mad.

Whoever said writing was easy? But reading was. The public consumed books, magazines and newspapers in unprecedented numbers. What better way to spend an evening than settling back with a book in a comfortable armchair with the wireless or gramophone playing in the background?

Lewis Baumer – the cigarette.

10

Paint Me a Picture

'Art is the only way to run away without leaving home.'

(Twyla Tharp)

In the dining-rooms of London's finest homes portraits of long forgotten ancestors stared down, whilst in the attics and basements of Hackney and Kilburn prints and samplers helped hide the damp patches on the walls. London was a leading centre of the art world but Londoners were a pretty conservative lot on the whole. They didn't like foreign food that had been 'mucked about' and they certainly didn't take to pictures or paintings they didn't understand. Post Impressionism and Vorticism might have been all the rage with those 'in the know', but the average man in the street wanted something easier on the eye. The grand, languid style of the Edwardian era survived, particularly in society portraiture. Photography had failed to stem the great and the good wanting their image recorded for posterity. Realistic representations of London low life and aggressive abstracts were also to be seen in the influential galleries of Bond Street and Mayfair. The summer exhibition at the Royal Academy remained an important event in the social calendar, but it was a less powerful influence than it had been during the second half of the nineteenth century.

Whilst working artists had long been associated with Chelsea and Hampstead, their studios were dotted all over the capital. Artists tended to be viewed with suspicion, fascination and grudging envy by Middle England. They wore their hair long, dressed in outlandish clothes and were bracketed with the acting profession in terms of behaviour and morals. Augustus John, holding forth in the Café Royal, epitomised the public view of the dissolute artist.

Portraiture

For the commercially aware artist, portraiture offered the fastest escape from the freezing garret. The ability to produce a good likeness usually ensured regular commissions. For the best in this genre, fame and fortune awaited. There was constant demand from the aristocracy, politicians and, increasingly, the captains of industry. Then there were their wives, daughters and even mistresses. The arch exponent of society portraiture before the war was John Singer Sargent who lived in Tite Street, Chelsea. His works were generally sympathetic to the sitter. He was able to convey character and mannerisms seemingly with a single flick of his brush. His subjects are recorded flatteringly and at ease, in what Walter Sickert described as 'the wriggle and chiffon school of portraiture'. By the twenties, nearing the end of his life, Sargent stated he was tired of producing these extremely well paid 'mugs'. This didn't stop him exhibiting two such works in 1922, including his portait of the Countess of Rocksavage. His last subject, exhibited at the Royal Academy after his death in 1925, was the redoubtable Marchioness Curzon. She was born Grace Elvina Hinds in Alabama and was one of a line of 'Southern Belles' to captivate London society. On the death of her first husband she married George Curzon, 1st Marquess of Kedleston, a former Viceroy of India and current Foreign Minister. Although in her mid-forties, Sargent captured her continuing wistful beauty.

Not only was society portraiture very lucrative, the foremost exponents tended to end up with a knighthood. John Lavery, Oswald Birley and William Nicholson were all eventually ennobled. Ambrose McEvoy also returned to portraiture late in his career, when in 1925 he exhibited works featuring Meraud Guinness and the singer John McCormack.

The Belfast-born artist, John Lavery, who lived in Cromwell Place, was already in his sixties by the time he was elected to the Royal Academy in 1921. He had been an official government artist during the war, and in 1920 he painted Admiral Sir David Beatty reading the terms of the armistice to German delegates aboard the *Queen Elizabeth*. He always maintained that a good artist should be capable of painting any subject but, increasingly, he was concentrating on portraiture. He was attacked by Joseph Pennell in 1926 as having forsaken his fellow artists and 'was in league with money'. 'Still,' he added witheringly, 'doing millionaires, surrounded by their millions was not bad.' Certainly many of his subjects shown at the Royal Academy could be identified in *Debrett's*. He also had a beautiful American wife Hazel who, in fairness, was his most popular model. She stares out at us across the years, elegant in fabulous gowns and

Mrs S. B. M. Lewis, wife of Spedan Lewis, by John St Helier Lander.

with the complexion of a porcelain doll. Like Sargent, Lavery's portraits tended to be flattering, but more dramatic. Undeterred by sniping comments, Lavery embarked on a series of lavish interiors, where the human figure was secondary to the furnishings. His interest in racing was in evidence in his much admired painting of the jockeys' changing room at Ascot. He returned to this theme with the weighing in of the Derby's winning jockey in 1924.

John St Helier Lander took his name from his birthplace in Jersey. Although largely forgotten today, he was amongst the most fashionable portrait artists of the twenties. He worked from his home and studio in Kensington. In 1923 he was commissioned to paint the Prince of Wales and chose to capture him dressed in polo kit. The painting was widely acclaimed and, subsequently, won a medal at the Paris Salon. In the same year he painted the then Lady Elizabeth Bowes-Lyon, who was to become our Queen and, later, the Queen Mother.

Oswald Birley, who lived in Wellington Road, NW8, was also at the height of his powers by the 1920s. Born in New Zealand, he was influenced by Sargent and churned out paintings of the great and the good, culminating in his portrait of the King, exhibited at the Royal Academy in 1929. At least William Nicholson, whilst still painting in the Edwardian manner, was also involved with design for the theatre, including the original set for *Peter Pan*.

The Camden Town Group

The one London school of art that refers to a specific area is the Camden Town Group. Although disbanded in 1919, its surviving members continued painting through the 1920s. It was the tragic death in 1918 of two of the group's leading members from Spanish flu that helped to accelerate its demise. Charles Ginner was taken ill and his friend and fellow artist Harold Gilman went to nurse him and also contracted the lethal flu. Sadly, they both died. Tragedy seemed to haunt the group as in 1914 Spencer Gore, a founder member, had died of pneumonia. The group had been formed to show London and its less fashionable streets in stark realism. It was Walter Sickert, whose dark, moody glimpses of London's seamier side caught the imagination of the public and influential collectors, who gained greater renown. He sold many of his works through the Conalghi dealers from their premises at 144 New Bond Street. Robert Bevan, who died in 1925, was also a founder member of the group. He is remembered particularly for his paintings of scrawny cab horses, all the more evocative because it was a part of London life that was fast disappearing. A memorial exhibition of his work was held at the Goupil Gallery in 1926. It was left to William Ratcliffe, a lesser-known member of the group, to stay true to its original principles, recording life on the streets close to his home in Belsize Park.

Percy Wyndham Lewis remained the major figure for those who embraced the abstract scene. His avant-garde style was based on angular, machine-like formations and his talent was acknowledged by his representation in a number of public collections, including the Tate Gallery. Christopher Nevison was another artist at the cutting edge of contemporary taste. He had also been an official war artist and was one of the first to record air combat. Early in his career, he was influenced by Cubism and Futurism. His jagged forms were challenging for the layman, but by 1925 his style had softened somewhat and his work became less radical.

Augustus John

Although highly regarded as a major artist during much of his lifetime, it is for his outlandish lifestyle that Augustus John is mainly remembered today. He was looked on as the ultimate bohemian with his constant womanising, including his well publicised *ménage à trois*. During the 1920s, he divided much of his time between his country home and his London house in Mallord Street, Chelsea. Although already in his forties, he continued to exude a dangerous magnetism, which proved irresistible to women of all ages. His long, tousled hair, beard and unconventional clothes were at odds with the dress and style of his peers. He had charisma, charm and talent. What was a lady to do? Lady Ottoline Morrell had no doubts. Although eight years his senior, she joined the ranks of women who became his lover. She was one of the leading society hostesses of her day. She devoted her

Augustus John and friends at the Café Royal.

life to the arts and artists. Some more than others! She was the wife of Philip Morrell, the Liberal MP, and they entertained on a grand scale from their home in Bedford Square and their country pad, Garsington Manor near Oxford. The couple enjoyed what was known as an open marriage. He sired several illegitimate children who were welcomed into the marital home, whilst Ottoline lined up a premier list of lovers, including Roger Fry and Bertrand Russell. The Morrells' lavish and quirky lifestyle took its toll on their finances and they were forced to downsize to a more modest home in Gower Street in 1927. Some of John's portraits (few of which were commissioned) bordered on caricature, but Lady Ottoline was reported to be delighted with the result of his work. He captured her in a distinctly unflattering light, emphasising her jutting jaw-line. For some time it took pride of place in the drawing-room of Garsington.

In 1926, Augustus staged a joint exhibition with his sister, Gwen, at the new Chenil Gallery. Their work (and personalities) were in stark contrast. In character and painting, he was loud, exuberant and larger than life. Gwen was withdrawn and her work largely confined to passive tones. Today it is her work that is more highly regarded and fetches huge sums at auction. Even her affair and infatuation with Rodin has left her brother's love life of less interest to a modern public. Whilst undoubtedly Augustus John completed several important works, including portraits of T. E. Lawrence and George Bernard Shaw, his stock has fallen from the heights he enjoyed in the 1920s. He was, perhaps, the first example of the 'celebrity' artist.

Hannah Gluckstein

Another outlandish artist was Hannah Gluckstein. She was the daughter of the fabulously wealthy Joseph Gluckstein, a member of the Joe Lyons catering empire. Her decision to become a professional artist caused her family considerable upset. This in spite of the fact that her American mother had been an opera singer. Their real hurt came in Hannah's overtly lesbian lifestyle. Her lovers included the florist Constance Spry. She drew further attention to herself by dressing as a man, even having her hair cut at a Bond Street barbers. Her androgynous style was widely imitated and later became an icon of high fashion. Although she studied briefly at the St John's School of Art alongside Alfred Munnings, she remained largely self taught. She scorned the Royal Academy and insisted on only showing her work in solo exhibitions. This somewhat arrogant approach was doubtless helped by her financial security. Her work was endorsed by the trend-setting designer Syrie Maugham. Although married to the writer Somerset Maugham, they spent much of their lives apart, allowing Syrie to develop her business. It was Syrie who first introduced and popularised rooms decorated in shades of white, and Gluck's stark paintings provided a perfect contrast.

In 1929 the Fine Art Society in Bond Street held an exhibition of forty works by Gluck, of which thirty were sold. She specialised in flower paintings, prompted in part by her association with Constance Spry. She was also an extremely penetrating portraitist where no facial characteristics, no matter how unflattering, escaped her eye. Gluck lived in considerable style in Hampstead and remained a free spirit until her death in 1976.

It is interesting to note that the Fine Art Society championed lesser known artists as well as the contemporary giants. In May 1920, the Australian-born artist Ida Outhwaite exhibited some of her delightful fairy and elves water colours. In 1922 Lamorna Birch, a regular exhibitor at the gallery, showed a number of Cornish scenes. Relatively unknown artist Avril Burleigh sold six water colours in 1925 for a combined total of £49. It is another artist, also largely forgotten today, who perhaps best represented the archetypal 1920s look. Lewis Baumer produced a series of 'stunners' with their translucent make up, button lips and bored expressions. His work appeared regularly in *Punch* and the *Tatler*, capturing the very spirit of the age. He also exhibited studies of his wife and daughter Priscilla at the Royal Academy in 1925. The following year he captured Noel Streatfeild, the well-known author. Baumer's paintings sold for as little as four guineas (in 1924) when exhibiting at the Fine Art Society. His picture posing the dilemma 'to bob or not to bob' meanwhile fetched ten guineas.

Although not a major figure of the art world, Lewis Baumer perhaps best represents the age with his portrayals of young flappers.

The illustrators

Illustrators like Baumer were an important part of the London art scene. Two leading illustrators of the time were Arthur Rackham and Ernest Shepard. They differed in style and yet both had the ability to gloriously illustrate books written by others.

Arthur Rackham

Arthur Rackham was already well into middle age by the start of the twenties. He represented not so much an Edwardian, but rather a Victorian influence. His amazingly detailed drawings and watercolours owed more to Cruikshank with their dark, almost threatening moodiness and yet he remained popular with both children and their parents. He created a fantasy world of hob goblins and elves. Tangled roots melded into human forms. Born into a lower middle-class south London family, he was a part-time student at the London School of Art, where he went after work. His wife Edyth was his guiding force, and she encouraged him to explore his fantasy world. His illustrations of the Brothers Grimm launched him on his way and by 1920 he was making regular promotional visits to the States. Improvements in colour printing allowed him greater scope. A disappointing reaction to an exhibition at the Leicester Galleries was followed by acclaim for his illustrations for Irish fairy-tales, which included sixteen colour plates. By 1926 he was producing memorable images for the publication of an illustrated version of *The Tempest*. That same year, he exhibited *The Little Stepdaughters* from Grimms' fairy-tales at the Royal Academy. Rackham was by now able to cherry pick books he wished to illustrate. For a time he tempered his style, softening the images somewhat, but his place as one of the great illustrators was assured. He continued working from his Primrose Hill studios until his death in 1939. One of his last projects was to illustrate Kenneth Grahame's *Wind in the Willows*.

Ernest Shepard

Ernest Shepard was born in St John's Wood in 1879. Already a successful contributor to *Punch*, and the illustrator of *David Copperfield* and *Tom Brown's Schooldays*, he had begun to exhibit at the Royal Academy by the outbreak of war. Although holding few recognised qualifications, he gained a commission and enjoyed 'a good war'. He saw action in Ypres, Arras and the Somme and was awarded the Military Cross. He continued sending illustrations to *Punch* during hostilities. He was discharged having achieved the rank of major. On his return to civvy street, Shepard was thrilled to be asked by the editor of *Punch* to join 'the table'. He was now not only a regular member of staff, but one of the few who met each month to decide which political cartoons were to be included in the next issue. The regular income and the security this brought allowed Shepard to improve the quality of his work. One of 'the table' members was E. V. Lucas, chairman of the publishers, Methuen. Lucas was a friend of A. A. Milne, who had himself previously been assistant editor of *Punch*. Milne had written some children's verses called *When We Were Young* and Lucas persuaded the editor of *Punch* to publish some of them. Although Milne didn't show much enthusiasm, Shepard worked on a series illustrating the verses. These appeared in *Punch* during the early months of 1924. They were well received and Milne then commissioned Ernest Shepard to illustrate the book bearing the same title, which had rapturous reviews. It was reprinted four times.

The following year, A. A. Milne bought a lovely, small estate in Sussex. It was there with his son, Christopher Robin, that the idea for *Winnie the Pooh* was born. Shepard was invited down to Cotchford Farm, so that he could try and interpret the make-believe world being formed in Milne's mind. It was vital that he should understand the characters the author wanted to project. Shepard took particular care in his sympathetic treatment of Christopher Robin and the little bear. *Winnie the Pooh* was published in 1926. The following year came *Now We Are Six* and in 1928 the amazingly successful *House at Pooh Corner*. It is astonishing that such a deep understanding developed between author and artist, when on a personal level they were never close. The Pooh books were eventually viewed as something of a millstone by Milne, who could never achieve the recognition he sought for his adult books. For Shepard, Pooh remained important for the rest of his life. He continued creating new illustrations for the stories and reworking existing examples. By the time his wife died in 1927, Shepard was experiencing financial difficulties. In spite of the overwhelming success of the Pooh books, he was forced to sell many of the original illustrations for as little as £5. Those same works go under the hammer today for many thousands of pounds!

Mabel Lucie Attwell

Of the many other talented book illustrators in the 1920s, Mabel Lucie Attwell is perhaps the most loved. Born in the East End in 1879, she was already a household name by the twenties. Like many other successful artists, she had little formal training, having failed to complete courses at either Regent or Heatherley's schools of art. Her talent for producing illustrations of adorable, chubby children soon won her recognition. Her work appeared regularly in the *Bystander* and *Tatler*. She also produced greetings cards for Valentine's Day. She was one of the first artists to have her work licensed and produced over a wide variety of commercial products, including posters, plaques and figurines. Although criticized for producing a production line of unchallenging, winsome, cheeky children, the public continued to love her work, which still has a definite appeal today. Strangely, Attwell was capable of producing work of an extremely sensitive nature, as witnessed in her illustrations for *Peter Pan and Wendy*, published in 1921. The *Boo Boo* books were best-sellers, as was her *Baby's Book* a year later. She was the artist equivalent of the author Enid Blyton, pilloried by the critics but loved by the great British public. The world was tough enough for most and what was wrong with producing a sentimentalised view of childhood? Attwell's popularity blossomed during the twenties, with the publication of her *Annual* from 1922 to 1974, ten years after her death. She was a most prolific artist and it is perhaps the cosy familiarity of her work that has taken its toll on her reputation.

Londoners of the 1920s were well served with such a wide variety of styles and choices. From grand and serious artists to commercial illustrators, they helped convey, in a subtle way, the time and place that photography was unable to do. As Pablo Picasso said, 'Painting is just another way of keeping a diary'.

A prize exhibit at the Royal Academy. Who cares about the pictures?

Savoy Hotel entrance.

11

Scandal

'*Scandal is what one half of the world takes pleasure in inventing and the other half believes.*'

(Paul Chatfield)

It's true. We all love a scandal as long as it doesn't impact on our own lives. London has always had more than its share of the macabre, bizarre and downright shocking. It's a pressure cooker and each day it disgorges a stream of indiscretions, greed and villainy. The 1920s was certainly no exception.

Trouble at the Savoy

Murders, of course, always hit the headlines. When the dirty deed takes place in the Savoy Hotel and involves wealthy foreigners and sex, the interest reaches boiling point. The trial of Marguerite Fahmy was predictably sensational. For once the British cast aside their traditional distrust of the French. Here, seemingly, was an attractive young French woman who had been subjected to outrageous humiliation by a playboy prince, a dissolute Egyptian, Prince Ali Kamel Fahmy Bey. Marguerite had converted to Islam in order to marry him, but from the outset the marriage was doomed. The prince showed more interest in his male secretary whilst subjecting her to perverted sexual practices. Middle England drew in a collective breath of shock and waited for further revelations. The year was 1923. The couple were seen having a violent argument in the Savoy restaurant, having spent the evening at the theatre watching Evelyn Laye starring in *The Merry*

Widow (you couldn't make it up!). They moved on to the ballroom where the Savoy Havana Band were playing, before returning to their luxury suite. At two o'clock the following morning, a night porter heard three shots and found the prince lying dead.

Defended by Sir Edward Marshall Hall, Marguerite was acquitted

The dark and alluring Marguerite Fahmy, but was she as sweet and innocent as she claimed?

by the jury in less than an hour. They had been fed in minute detail the degrading treatment Marguerite had been forced to endure. In his summing up, the judge said, 'We in this country put our women on a pedestal; in Egypt they have not the same views.' The defence had been so racially motivated that it led to a diplomatic protest from the Egyptian Embassy.

After the trial, views began to change somewhat. Marguerite, who was ten years older than her husband, was found to have given birth to an illegitimate child when she was just fifteen. It was reported that she had been a prostitute in Paris and was just a gold digger. It did her no good. Fahmy had not made a will and, despite her best efforts, she inherited nothing. The great British public felt vindicated. True, for a time they had fallen for her sob story, but it just underlined the widely held view that all foreigners were distinctly suspect.

The Maltby case

At least British murderers were capable of doing the decent thing when confronted. Cecil Maltby lived above his tailor's shop in Park Road, Regent's Park. An expensive address for a business that was going through difficult times in 1922. Presumably life seemed a little better when Alice Middleton moved in with the forty-seven-year-old. Her husband was a merchant seaman who was safely away in the Far East. Unexpectedly, he arrived home to find her gone without trace. He reported her missing and the police learned that she had been linked to Maltby. He behaved very oddly when they called at his shop and refused them entry. They returned with a search warrant and forced their way in, only to hear a shot. They found Maltby dead in a bedroom. In the bathroom was the decomposed body of Middleton. There was a note pinned to the sheet covering her. It read: 'In memory to my darling Pat who committed suicide on 24th August 1922'. (Pat being his pet name for her.) It's difficult to shoot yourself three times in the back. The coroner recorded a verdict of murder. The papers had given the case blanket coverage but there were other outrages swirling around.

A murderous rivalry

The British often attempt to take the moral high ground when it comes to prostitution. In London it has invariably been controlled by foreigners, but most of the punters were, of course, home grown. In the early twenties two colourful characters vied for supremacy and this was eventually to end in murder. Juan Antonio Castanar was a good-looking Spaniard who was an expert tango dancer. At one stage he was even associated with the great Anna Pavlova. Castanar ran a dance school in Archer Street, which acted as a front enabling him to sell gullible girls, ostensibly to join dance troupes on the continent. He also arranged marriages of convenience for foreign women, enabling them to acquire a British passport, which allowed them to work on the streets of Soho. His activities were so lucrative that he was frequently seen driving around the West End in his Rolls-Royce.

His rival, and another major player, was an interesting character, Cosimir Michletti. He was an extremely handsome Algerian. He was softly spoken, with a mild manner and thought by many to be charming on first meeting. He could also fight with the savagery of a tiger if crossed or upset. He was known as 'The Assassin', a man to be feared. The men's rivalry extended to a very real personal animosity. This culminated in a confrontation at the 43 Club in Old Compton Street, when Michletti savagely slashed the Spaniard's face. There followed a series of gang fights and murders, which proved their undoing as they were both deported. They found themselves stranded in Paris and business pickings were poor. Castanar was planning a return to London but he wanted Michletti silenced for good. He shot the Algerian dead, but was arrested before making his escape across the Channel and sent to Devil's Island, opening up a vacancy for the control of prostitution in London.

Captain Leslie Barker

Whilst gangsters were interesting, the most sensational scandal of 1929 saw the circulation of the London and national dailies soar. The most bizarre trial of the decade involved Captain (sometimes known as Colonel) Leslie Barker. He was arrested at the Regent Palace Hotel in February 1929, having failed to appear for a bankruptcy hearing scheduled for the previous December. Barker, who claimed to have been highly decorated for his war service, had a reputation for being a useful boxer and something of a womaniser. Whisked off to Brixton prison, he was subjected to a routine medical examination. The doctor was in for a nasty shock. Leslie Barker was a woman! Although he was separated from his wife, she was also reported to be shocked and dazed. They had shared a marital bed together for five years and she had never suspected, their rather unusual marital arrangements being attributed to his supposed war wounds. The popular press could hardly contain their glee as more revelations were aired. Barker, born Lilian Irma Valerie Barker, had enjoyed an absolutely normal upbringing. As a young woman she had shown a great interest in horses and worked for a time as a trainer. In 1918 she married Australian Lieutenant Harold Arkell-Smith. The marriage lasted only a matter of weeks. She then formed a relationship with another Australian, Ernest Pearle-Crouch, with whom she had two children. However, by 1923 she emerged as Colonel Leslie Barker. In his male guise he won the heart of Elfrida Haward and the approval of her parents. Married life didn't run quite so smoothly as Barker drifted in and out of a variety of jobs. Boxing manager, café owner and farm manager were just a few. Showing an alarming inability to stick with anything for any length of time, Barker then became involved with the fascist movement, organising boxing training for members. In 1927 Barker was charged with being in possession of a firearm with a forged certificate. He was found not guilty, helped perhaps by turning up in court with his eyes covered in bandages claiming he had been blinded in the war. It was all too much for Elfrida and she eventually left her husband. The authorities were unsure what charges to bring and finally settled on perjury. Barker was sentenced to nine months in Holloway. The whole of London was fascinated. Transvestite was a word few had heard of before. The *Daily Mail*, rarely missing a trick where a sensational storyline was on offer, ran 'My Own Story' by Captain Leslie Barker. It was pretty tame stuff but it kept the interest going. Upon release, Barker continued living as a man with a variety of female partners. He worked for a time as a butler before retiring to Suffolk and serving in the Home Guard before dying in 1960.

Horatio Bottomley

Whilst the gruesome and salacious grab the headlines there were other scandals with far more long-term consequences. Horatio Bottomley was in every sense a larger-than-life character. A lover of excess in everything, he weighed in at over seventeen stones. By his mid thirties he was said to be worth £3 million (a massive sum at today's values). On the downside, he had picked up over sixty writs for bankruptcy. He was a chancer with a golden tongue. During the war he spoke at recruitment rallies, keeping much of the gate proceeds for himself. He continued to expand his business interests, which already included the patriotic magazine *John Bull*. He periodically ran competitions naming non-existent winners and pocketing the funds collected as entrance money. He continued to live a charmed life, twice being acquitted of fraud. He had a reputation for being able to sweet talk his way out of any situation. Due to the crippling costs of the war, the government elected to issue a series of Victory Bonds in 1919. At a cost of £5 these were out of reach of much of the population. Bottomley immediately spotted an opportunity. Promoting himself as 'the people's friend', he introduced a scheme whereby the poorer members of society could buy a fifth of a bond for £1. He promised to buy bonds on their behalf and place them in the hands of trustees. He also promised their capital would remain intact and he would also pay interest on their investment. In addition, they could claim their money back for full refund, if required. There appeared to be no risk. Bottomley had become a popular national figure, with his rabble-rousing oratory during the war. So popular, he had been elected to Parliament as an independent MP for Hackney South in 1918. To most people he appeared a pillar of society. He was not.

Apart from being a crook, Bottomley was totally disorganised and for much of the time his mind was blurred by excessive drinking. Within days of its launch, it was obvious that the scheme was going to be a massive success. The sheer volume of money being deposited required an efficient method of record keeping. Bottomley had only recruited a handful of untrained clerks. There were no control systems in place. It was chaos. Some of the clerks saw the possibility of pocketing large sums for themselves. At the height of the scheme's popularity the 'Victory Club' was receiving over £100,000 a day in cash. As well as mountains of cash, thousands of cheques were being added to the mix. He still hadn't bought any legitimate Victory Bonds, waiting patiently for the price to fall. The public had no inkling of this but trouble for Bottomley had started. Slowly, at first, letters went unanswered. A trickle turned to a stream as investors asked to have their money returned. No response. Murmurings of discontent. Bottomley finally stirred himself, investing in half a million Victory Bonds, which he was able to secure at a very keen price. He even returned some £150,000 of investors' money and assured everyone who would listen that his scheme was rock solid. It wasn't. The influx of investors dried up. Those requesting repayment had grown into a torrent. Bottomley had used the vast sums of money flowing in to pay off some existing debts and also to purchase a couple of newspapers. His racing stables also ate into his reserves, as did his string of mistresses. This was one situation that even Horatio Bottomley couldn't talk himself out of. He tried. Although he had robbed the very people he purported to help, he was not about to go quietly. At his trial he boomed that the sword of justice hanging on the wall behind the judge would fall if he were found guilty. It didn't. He was. On his release from jail in 1927, he made a few sad appearances at the Windmill Theatre. He continued appearing down the bill at second-rate music halls and died a broken man in 1933.

Clarence Hatry

Whilst Horatio Bottomley was a serious fraudster, his activities tended to only rob his investors individually of small amounts of money. His trick was to get hundreds of thousands involved. Clarence Hatry, although less well known, was one of the catalysts for the total collapse of the world economy in 1929. Born in 1888, he made money initially by arranging the transportation of eastern Europeans to the States. Moving on, he started investing in vending machines and cameras. Like Bottomley, he was a flamboyant character, a chancer, who took risks, went bust and rose again. Although he had already been bankrupt by the age of twenty, he was undeterred. He went into insurance, paying £60,000 for City Equitable, before selling it for a hefty £250,000. He acquired all the trappings of wealth: houses, racehorses and a yacht reckoned to be the second largest in the world at the time. He was now a superstar of the business world. By 1928, his companies were reckoned to have a turnover of several million pounds a month. He now sought to get control of the giant United Steel, which was said to account for about ten per cent of the UK's steel production. Unfortunately, he didn't have the £3 million he needed to secure the deal with the company, which was eventually to become British Steel. He was unstinting in his efforts to raise the money. He cooked his books, showing his organisation to be in rude health with a strong balance sheet. Still his connections in the City and the Bank of England held back. With the recklessness of a born gambler, he stupidly started forging share certificates (with worthless paper) in an attempt to borrow money to finance the deal. His vast empire, which included station photographic booths and an impressive range of investment companies, some chaired by august members of the aristocracy, collapsed. On inspection, his companies were shown to have a deficit of over £130 million.

With the fraud exposed, trading in the Hatry group was suspended on 20th September 1929. The stock market began to fall and news swept across the Atlantic. Nine days later saw the start of the Wall Street crash. Hatry was convicted at the Old Bailey and sentenced to fourteen years in jail, the first two to be of hard labour. From breaking the hearts of those who invested with him to breaking rocks was a savage fall from grace for a man who had only recently been lauded and courted by the rich and influential. Gone was his racing stable, his Mayfair house with its swimming pool on the roof and his yacht. Released after serving just seven years, he sought to reinvent himself, investing in a range of bookstores, including Hatchards. He died in 1965.

12

Food for Thought

'Eat with your fingers, drink with your nose.'
(Joseph Delteil)

For most Londoners, eating out was normally confined to a cup of tea and a slice of cake in a café. It was only the wealthy or aspiring who ventured into Soho or Covent Garden. Foreign food was generally viewed with suspicion. Londoners liked their food good and plain and not mucked about with. Most families sat down to a roast and two veg for Sunday lunch. The joint was then served cold on a Monday and the remains minced on Tuesday. It might even stretch to an Anglicised curry on Wednesday, and then when Friday came round it was time for a trip to the fishmongers.

A palace on every corner

One company above all others was responsible for making eating out an affordable and often exciting experience. J. Lyons & Co. was created by the Gluckstein brothers, Barnett Salmon and the English sounding Joe Lyons. They formed a dynasty that was going to dominate the catering trade for the first half of the century. The business was started before the war, and soon the white- and gold-fronted tea shops were scattered all over London and into the provinces. At one time, there were seven separate outlets along the length of Oxford Street. Prices were identical, no matter where the shops were located. The first Lyons Corner House had been built in Coventry Street before the war and was extended in 1922. Like Gordon Selfridge, Joe Lyons

147

One of the many restaurants at the Oxford Street Corner House.

wanted their customers to spend as much time as possible in their shops. To help encourage this, the Corner Houses were built like palaces. They were flamboyant, bringing a touch of glamour to people's lives. By 1928 the largest Corner House was built at the corner of Oxford Street and Tottenham Court Road, to add to their other huge outlet on the Strand. The new complex was capable of serving over 20,000 meals a day. It was built with marble columns, and huge murals lined the walls. The ground floor was given over to a giant food hall and delicatessen. A huge range was on offer laid out on counters and served by smartly uniformed staff. There were cakes, pastries, gateaux and their famous lemon meringue pies. Hams and cold meats were sliced for waiting customers. There were huge displays of cheeses, a salad bar and even hand-made chocolates at prices that many were tempted by. There was a sense of theatre about the whole presentation and, as a concept, it would not seem out of place today. The Corner Houses were built on four or five floors, each featuring a different type of restaurant. They ranged from cheap and cheerful self-service, including the salad bar on the top floor, to well presented meals served by smartly uniformed waiters. Each restaurant had its own band to supply suitable background music. It was a revelation for most people, bringing a touch of theatre and excitement to their lives. Joe Lyons tried to cover the needs of all diners and it was the largest catering organisation in Europe. They also ran some outlets under the Maison Lyons brand, which was very similar to the Corner House concept but run by a different management team. In Piccadilly, they had their Popular Café, which seated over 2,000.

Whilst the Corner House concept was difficult to compete with due to its sheer size and scope, the everyday tea room was a fiercely fought-over sector. Both ABC and Express Dairies ran popular tea rooms, although even here Joe Lyons was market leader, with his waitresses in their distinctive black and white uniforms, fondly known as 'Nippies'. Fullers were rather more up-market with their thirty outlets, whose rich, dark chocolate cakes gained legendary status. An early emergence of fast food arrived with Sandy's All British Sandwich Bar, which offered sixty choices of fillings for hungry office workers, whilst Alfredo's opened on Essex Road, Islington, selling the ultimate bacon sandwich. Still, Lyons continued to spread its sphere of activity to outside catering. Its buying

A Joe Lyons' 'Nippy', a familiar figure for generations to come.

power was enormous, allowing the company to cater for a wide range of social and sporting events, including Buckingham Palace garden parties, the Chelsea Flower Show and the Wimbledon Tennis Championships.

The Trocadero

Lyons had also moved into hotel ownership, but it is the Trocadero on Shaftesbury Avenue that is remembered with most affection. It was a huge, ornate building with restaurants or rooms set aside for functions on each of its floors. Its introduction of tea dances was amazingly popular and much copied. The company was one of the first to realise that live music drew the customers in. By the mid twenties the Trocadero had introduced cabaret suppers, many of which were produced by Charles Cochran, featuring new and established stars. The restaurants were also known for selling wine at very

Eating out and cabaret were important parts of the London social scene.

reasonable prices. They sold so much that they appointed their own wine buyer. Their list ran to over 500 choices in an attempt to indulge and satisfy their thirsty clientele.

Up-market eating

For the more adventurous or well heeled, London offered a huge range of restaurants covering an amazing choice of cuisines. Perhaps the first celebrity chef to appear in London was Marcel Boulestin. His 1925 book *The Conduct of the Kitchen* became a best-seller. A year later he opened his famous restaurant in Covent Garden. His slogan was 'good food should be the rule, not the exception.' The restaurant was decorated in the latest Art Deco style and soon was attracting the rich and famous. He concentrated on using fresh food purchased daily from the Central Market. There were many other restaurants catering for the top end of the market. The Connaught Rooms in Great Queen Street appealed to establishment figures, including royalty and leading politicians. It was also supported by the influential Freemasons. Frascati's in Oxford Street was well thought of, as was the Holborn in Kingsway. Romano's on the Strand attracted a rather more louche clientele and was run by the restaurant's former wine waiter. Several of London's best restaurants were run by men who had started in the trade at the very humblest level.

Not far from Marcel Boulestin's Covent Garden restaurant was Rules in Maiden Lane. It was, and remains, London's oldest restaurant. Bizarrely, the owner, Tom Bell, swapped his Paris restaurant for Rules, as the owner, Charles Rule, had tired of London and wanted to live in Paris, thus relinquishing ownership of the property that had been in his family's control for over a century at the time.

For those returning from the Raj there was a first opportunity to dine on authentic Indian food in London at Verraswamy's on Regent Street. This forerunner of Britain's favourite cuisine opened in 1926 and is still going strong today. Chinese restaurants, which had traditionally been situated in Limehouse, started migrating to the

Piping in the Haggis at The Savoy, St Andrew's Day 1923.

West End and Soho. Brilliant Chang, the infamous drug dealer, ran a restaurant at 107 Regent Street until he was forced to retreat again to the East End. There was already a smattering of Chinese restaurants in Gerrard Street, which has subsequently become known as China Town. Others were recorded in Shaftesbury Avenue, Dean Street, Greek Street, and there were several in Wardour Street.

In 1917, Abel Giandellini purchased a modest café in West Street. Shortly after opening he was joined by Mario Gallati as his *maître d'*. The restaurant soon found favour with the theatrical community who were playing the nearby theatres. The two men transformed this understated establishment into what is now probably London's most sought after restaurant, The Ivy. Gallati, later in life, went on to acquire some of London's best known and respected restaurants, including Á l'Ecu de France and Le Caprice.

Soho – global cuisine in one district

Many visitors from the provinces tended to stay in their hotels to eat, but for the more adventurous Soho offered hundreds of restaurants appealing to all tastes. Amongst the most popular was L'Escargot, which is still serving good food today. Built on the site of a famous cockfighting pit in Greek Street, it was owned by George Gaudin who managed to persuade the English that snails were indeed tasty. Kettner's also remains trading today, but not in a form that would be recognised by the twenties clientele. In those days it was popular for truly 'intimate dining' and discreet assignations in one of its upstairs private rooms. Similarly, Quo Vadis is still popular today. It was here in Dean Street that Karl Marx lodged for a time.

French restaurants were the best represented in Soho, but there were also Italian, Greek, Cypriot, Spanish, Jewish, Russian, Turkish and Chinese. A particular French favourite was Moulin d'Or at 27 Romilly Street, which tended to attract a rather bohemian clientele. Petit Savoyard served excellent food at 35 Greek Street, whilst Isola Bella was one of the most popular Italian outlets. It was at 15 Frith Street and its speciality Ravioli al Sugo had customers returning regularly. It was bouillabaisse that had people flocking to Beguinot's at 16 Old Compton Street. Here you were able to eat really tasty meals at a very reasonable price. Those looking for kosher food had a choice of Blooms, Sugarman's or Goody's Jewish Restaurant at 15 Berwick Street. Wheeler's started as a retail oyster bar and became a restaurant in 1929. It was owned by a Mr Walsh, who expanded his fish restaurants to include several other Soho landmarks over the coming years.

For those who wanted to eat away from their fashionable hotels but were put off by Soho's rather dubious reputation, there were still options. A safe bet was the Prince's Restaurant at 191 Piccadilly, which sported four bands and an ebony dance floor. Opposite was the traditional Hatchells, which occupied the site of the Old White Horse cellars. An interesting alternative would have been the Café Royal on Regent Street. It was partially rebuilt between 1923 and 1924 to conform with the redevelopment of Regent Street. On the ground floor, to the side of the luncheon bar and grill room, was the Domino Room. This continued to draw in the artistic community, including Augustus John and his acolytes. The Café Royal was reputed to have the best cellar in London and was unusual in that its management refused to have live music in its downstairs area. Upstairs, the Empire Room was used for special occasions, charity dinners and cabaret. The room was dominated by doors, each topped with decorative arches. Yellow walls on a bluish background were set off by grand arches of orange, whilst the huge doors glowed a polished brown. The Café Royal provided a suitable link to London's night-clubs, which covered a multitude of sins.

Night-clubbing

What is a night-club? A grand, luxurious setting where smart gentlemen in tailed suits spin their glamorous ladies round a dance floor? Or a smoke-filled room with mugs playing cards with a marked deck, whilst grim-faced gangsters and their brassy escorts look on? London could offer you both and everything in between and worse. Much worse!

Café de Paris

The most iconic night-club in London, until it was destroyed by a bomb in 1941, was the Café de Paris. Formerly the Elysée Restaurant, it was purchased by the theatrical agent George Foster. In an astute move he persuaded Martin Paulsen, the head waiter at the fashionable Embassy Club, to run his new venture. The Prince of Wales had promised Paulsen that if he ever ran his own club he would give it his support. He honoured that promise, and became a regular visitor from 1924. Where the prince went, others followed. Leading stars including Noel Coward, Fred Astaire and Marlene Dietrich starred in *Cabaret* there. The Café de Paris soon became the place to be seen. Coventry Street had previously been known for its lines of prostitutes. Now this two-tiered basement drew the great and the good like bees to honey. Approached through double glass doors, the décor was an exact replica of the Palm Court aboard the doomed liner, Lusitania. Entering the 'bridge' there was a central lobby with a view of the whole restaurant. Twin staircases, each of twenty-one steps, swooped down to the dance floor. Diners instinctively looked up to view every entrance. Gentlemen in tailed suits escorted their ladies to the tables allotted to them. Formal dress was essential to gain entry to the dance-floor area. The balcony was reserved for lesser mortals and those who chose to wear dinner jackets. The table immediately adjoining the dance floor at the bottom of the right-hand staircase was permanently reserved for His Royal Highness. The resident band was tucked into a recess under the bridge. It was a perfect venue for entertaining, impressing friends or for a budding romance. It also had a secret staircase, which ran from the balcony onto Rupert Street for discreet arrivals or getaways.

The Embassy Club

Previously, top society had favoured the Embassy Club situated at the Piccadilly end of Bond Street. A major draw there was Bert Ambrose and his orchestra. The Prince of Wales was a huge fan and was a regular visitor most Thursday evenings. He was normally preceded by his equerry, 'Fruity' Metcalfe, to ensure everything was in order. The Embassy had a small square dance floor just made for intimate, cheek-to-cheek contact. Bert Ambrose had returned from a trip to the States in 1922, when he was approached by Albert de Courville and offered over £300 a week to run a seven-piece band. Soon after, de Courville ran into severe money problems and he sold out to the well-known restaurateur Luigi. Problems between the new owner and Ambrose grew because Luigi would not allow live broadcasts to be made from the club. Ambrose knew that nationwide fame could only be achieved through recordings whose sales were boosted enormously by being heard on the wireless. To his frustration, his early records sold very poorly. Feeling Luigi was strangling his career, Ambrose again took off to New York to seek the recognition he felt he was due. Luigi pleaded with him to return. It took a telegram from the Prince of Wales, which said, 'The Embassy needs you – come back. Edward.' That really was an offer he couldn't afford to refuse. He stayed at the Embassy Club until 1927 when he was 'poached' to go and play at the Mayfair Hotel. This time he moved, not for money, but the chance to broadcast live, which opened up the opportunities for his long and successful recording career. In 1929 he recorded a number of legendary sessions including 'Thou Swell', 'I May be Wrong (But I Think You're Wonderful)', 'Love Me or Leave Me', and 'Button up Your Overcoat' with vocals by Lou Abelardo. He had a very English, rather lightweight voice. Pleasant enough, but lacking in emotion. It would be a couple more years before Al Bowlly took popular singing onto a completely new, elevated level. Despite the added competition and loss of Ambrose, the Embassy remained extremely popular. Who needed Bert Ambrose when Luigi regularly tossed clients 'double or nothing' for their bill?

Kate Meyrick – queen of clubs

Outside of the establishment clubs and hotels, half the excitement of visiting night-clubs was the slight whiff of danger. Licensing laws had changed in 1921, only allowing premises to serve drinks after hours provided food was served. Most establishments paid only lip service to the law, hence the possible police raids and tension adding to the occasion. The undoubted queen of London clubs was Kate Meyrick.

Kate Meyrick, the hostess with the mostest, pictured at The Silver Slipper Club with fashionable guests.

The daughter of an Irish doctor, she was abandoned by her husband leaving her to bring up six children. She answered an advertisement in April 1919 placed by George Dalton Murray stating 'fifty pounds wanted for partnership to run tea dances.' They set up Daltons Club in Leicester Square. It was soon referred to as 'an absolute sink of iniquity'. By January 1920 the club was in trouble and Mrs Meyrick was jailed for non payment of fines. It was not to be her last brush with the law. She moved on to run Brett's Dance Hall from a basement in Charing Cross Road. She was beginning to get the hang of things. She quickly expanded her stable of clubs to include the Cat Burglar's, the Silver Slipper in Regent Street, the Bunch of Keys and the Manhattan. Her most famous acquisition was the Proctor's Club, soon to be known as The 43. It was situated in Gerrard Street. She was described as a wispy little woman, who always had holes in her stockings and an old green shawl drawn across her shoulders. Contemporaries speak of the club being run with a real warmth and originality. Champagne starting at 30/- a bottle may not have been that unusual, but certainly helped bring the profits in. Ma, as she was known, sat just inside the door onto Gerrard Street, keeping an eye on the girl taking the entrance money. Regulars who were temporarily strapped for cash were often allowed in free, particularly if they brought in new, free-spending guests.

Unfortunately for Ma Meyrick, her prominence came to the attention of the home secretary, Sir William Joynson-Hicks. Hicks hated night-clubs. In fact, he hated most things that helped make life fun. Drink, sex, people enjoying themselves, foreigners and particularly blacks. The whole list of his prejudices had a common denominator – night-clubs! He set out to make life as difficult as possible and over sixty-five clubs were prosecuted over a four-year period for selling drinks after hours. Many that were closed down opened the following day under a different name. Between 1924 and 1928 The 43 stood alone in not being raided. It took an anonymous letter to the authorities, suggesting they looked into the affairs of a Sergeant Goddard of the Vice Squad. On pay of just £6.15 a week, he was running a sizeable car and found to have £12,000 in a deposit account. The money had been obtained from Ma and the owner of Uncle's Club in Albemarle Street. He and Ma Meyrick were given fifteen-month sentences, whilst the sergeant went down for an eighteen-month spell of hard labour. Although Ma Meyrick had served several terms in jail, this sentence took its toll on her and she died in the early thirties, leaving under £1,000. Yet, in her prime, the clubs had been so profitable that she was able to send her two sons to Harrow and her daughters to Roedean. It was estimated that the Silver Slipper was showing weekly profits in excess of £500 and The 43 would regularly take over £600 a night. For some years she was given sound financial advice by the well-known investor Sir Alfred Lowenstein, and was said to be worth over £500,000. When he died in 1928 her own choice of investments haemorrhaged money. She died in 1933, having served two more prison sentences. During one of her enforced 'holidays', Evelyn Waugh commented in his diary, 'Tony and I went to The 43, where Miss Meyrick is carrying on her mother's place exactly the same as ever.' Two of Ma's daughters did very well for themselves, marrying into the aristocracy. Ma died aged fifty-six at the home of her son-in-law, Lord Kinnoull. Dance bands throughout the West End staged a two-minute silence in memory of a true eccentric.

With the home secretary in full flow, nowhere was safe. Even the Kit-Kat Club, a favourite haunt of the Prince of Wales, was raided. Clubs started instigating escape routes for their clients. Alarm systems were introduced to warn of impending raids. A febrile atmosphere built up. Going to night-clubs was so exciting!

It would seem that the Prince of Wales spent most evenings in West End clubs. Pops in Soho Square was another favourite, as was the fashionable Chez Henri in Long Acre, where Charlie Kunz entertained on his piano. The Lido Club in Newman Street was best known for its excellent cabaret. Clubs were in fashion as never before. Ivor Novello opened the 50/50 Club whose name conveyed a certain sexual ambivalence. The Gargoyle Club in Meard Street was supposedly opened by its founder, David Tennant, because he wanted somewhere to dance with his girlfriend, the actress Hermione Baddeley. Here was a club with a difference, seeking to bring London's social elite and the artistic community together. Prices were kept low to encourage struggling painters, writers, poets and musicians. Many were excused the seven-guinea subscription required of the more establishment figures. Members included Somerset

Maugham, Arnold Bennett and members of the Rothschild and Guinness dynasties. Part of the décor was undertaken by Henri Matisse and it was soon reckoned to be the most chic club in London.

The other side of the coin

By no means all clubs set out to attract the talented, moneyed and well connected. At the bottom of the club scene there were hundreds of spielers and dives run by crooks who, in turn, had to pay their dues to the Sabini gang. *John Bull* magazine railed against Soho clubs 'selling whisky of the vilest quality for 2/6 per nip'. It claimed that the Shaftesbury Club in Great Earl Street was not a club at all, but a haven for thieves and underworld women. The Radio Club was a single room in Old Compton Street where crowds gathered to drink after hours. Similar places, like the Premier Club, were close by. Hardly a basement or attic in Soho was not in use, and by 1926 *John Bull* had gone into overdrive about Jack Kitten's café in Seven Dials, which was known as 'The Black Café'. The magazine thundered, 'A TERRIBLE NEGRO HAUNT, THE KITTEN AND THE MICE; CAFÉ MUST BE CLOSED.' It reported 'one of the most sickening sights witnessed everyday in this place is the spectacle of white women shamelessly consorting with black men!' Outraged, the owner sued Odhams Press. He was wasting his time. Costs were awarded against him and Kitten was declared bankrupt. His application for discharge was refused. 'He was,' said the judge, 'the cause of his own misfortune by bringing a frivolous action.' The Falstaff in Oxford Street was described as being the wickedest place in London. Here, all the thieves and whores of London came to spend their money. Stolen goods were exchanged, jobs planned. Women walked across the crowded room naked for a ten-bob bet. There were no rules, it bristled with an air of barely suppressed violence. The Sabini gang moved in. They wanted more of the take. They smashed the place up and it closed.

So, whilst the prince, his pals and the wealthy dined and danced at their fashionable clubs, just around the corner lurked another London. Brothels, clip joints, groups of men huddled in darkened spielers. Sometimes, the two sides ventured into each other's territory in an uneasy alliance, in the joint pursuit of pleasure.

13

A Racing Certainty

*'A racehorse is an animal that can take several thousand people for a ride at
the same time.'*

(Author unknown)

The sport of kings actually appealed to the working man just as
much as the aristocracy. Much of the appeal for those attending a
race meeting was the heady mix of spectators. Mixing at a distance,
that is, without exactly rubbing shoulders. Sandown Park was the
first course to introduce enclosures. It was 'a place where a man could
take his ladies without fear of their hearing coarse language or
witnessing uncouth behaviour!' A form of social apartheid, according
to a contemporary diarist.

Londoners loved their racing. As well as Sandown they had easy
access to Kempton Park, Alexandra Palace, Hurst Park, plus Epsom
and Ascot. Derby Day had massive crowds converging on Epsom
from early morning. This was London's day out. They spread themselves
over the Downs, having travelled in double-decker buses, charabancs,
spluttering cars, and some still by pony and trap. There were gypsies
with skin like leather, peering into crystal balls, shady looking characters
selling tips and claiming to be 'in the know'. Bookies shouted the
odds, whilst tick-tack men waved their arms as if they were controlled
by some outside force. Little had changed since William Powell Frith
captured the chaos of Derby Day in his 1858 painting.

Whilst Derby Day was for ordinary Londoners, Royal Ascot was
the highlight of the London social scene. Each day, the royal coach
procession arrived on the course from Windsor. There were outriders
dressed in vivid scarlet and gold uniforms. Postillions sporting grey

wigs and jockey caps. The gentlemen raised their top hats, whilst the ladies in all their finery curtsied. The royal box was decorated with an array of hydrangeas, whilst the royal enclosure was festooned with colourful rhododendrons. The feeling projected by Royal Ascot was of continuity, power and national pride. Change was on the way, but it must wait for another day.

Racing had become so popular that *Sporting Life* was selling over a hundred thousand copies a day. The paper provided form guides and details of the going. Photographs captured the excitement of a close finish or a heavy fall. Copies could be found in pubs, barbers and hotels. The daily newspapers were devoting more space to racing, and for major events special correspondents were assigned to find stories of human interest. The *nom de plumes* of the racing experts still exist in most of today's papers. Hotspur in the *Telegraph*, Robin Goodfellow in the *Mail* and the Scout in the *Express*. Even the *Communist Daily Worker* allowed its readers to indulge in a little private enterprise. Increasingly, proprietors and editors realised the importance of their racing journalists. They benefited by generally being rather well paid with salaries of up to £1,100 a year. Top jockeys, like Steve Donoghue, had become celebrities and, in his case, he started contributing to a column for the *London Evening Standard*'s midday edition in 1927.

Despite the space given over to racing in the press, betting off course was illegal unless you had a credit account with a bookmaker. Bookies' runners standing on street corners were a familiar sight right across London. There was a feeling amongst the establishment that gambling for the working man was dangerous and should be discouraged.

As with prohibition in the States, this only had the effect of increasing betting demand. It was estimated that there were 800 street bookies across London in 1928. Punters tended to bring their cash stakes wrapped in a slip of paper listing their selection. Most used nicknames, making it more difficult to trace them if the runner was arrested. Having to pay the runners reduced the bookies' profits, but it was better for them than having no business at all. They were very ingenious in recruiting not just runners, but tradesmen like milkmen and bakers, who were making regular household deliveries. Many publicans encouraged bookmakers to use their premises as it helped swell their takings. In addition to runners, look-outs had to be employed as the police were often active in trying to stop the trade. Winnings were normally paid the day following the race. As telephones were more widely used, kiosks were often the venue chosen for pay-outs. In 1921, a war office clerk was arrested for running a book in the Household Cavalry Brigade canteen. Credit bookmakers were perfectly legal but tended to deal with the relatively well-to-do who ran their own bank accounts. Bookies advertised in the racing press, promising absolute discretion. The larger organisations emphasised their financial stability as it was not unknown for bookies 'to do a runner'.

Trouble at the track

Whilst for the most part a day at the races offered a pleasant outing, intimidation and violence were seldom far away. Racecourse gangs offering bookies protection were fighting for control.

The Sabini brothers

The Sabini brothers from Clerkenwell were the major force; they were also powerful enforcers of West End gambling haunts. Their leader, Darby Sabini, was reputed to have direct links with the Mafia. He was assisted by his brothers, Harry-Boy, Fred and George. Their protection amounted to little more than demanding money with menaces. Once when they appeared in court, a judge, showing off his linguistic skills, addressed them in Italian, only to be met with blank stares. These were Anglicised Italians, who spoke with cockney accents. Darby left school at thirteen. A tough youngster, he was reckoned to be a genuine boxing prospect. Darby was too smart. If there was any fighting he wanted to ensure it was one-sided. The gang was violent and ruthless. The protection it offered racecourse bookies was bizarre. They had to pay out for everything, from the chalk required to write up the odds to the stools they stood on. They had to pay 2/6 for a sheet listing the runners, money for the sponges to wipe their boards, even water to wet the sponge. Any bookie refusing to pay would have his pitch surrounded by the gang who would block potential punters. Alternatively, the gang would start fights, in fact resort to anything to make sure the offending bookie took no money. Darby had well-oiled connections with the 'Flying Squad' so he tended not to get too much trouble from the police. The net result was an extremely lucrative trade, which could amount to a take of up to £15,000 on Derby Day.

The Sabinis, known as 'the Italian mob', recruited a large Jewish intake as they widened their sphere of influence. Trouble was brewing. The Cortesi brothers, Enrico, Paul, Augustus and George, known as 'the Frenchies', formed a breakaway from the Sabinis and were joined by some of the Jewish boys. The new outfit attempted to hijack the Sabinis' takings after a day's racing at Kempton Park in the autumn of 1922. Retribution was swift and savage. Harry Sabini was convicted of an assault on George Cortesi and five of the Sabini gang were charged with attempted murder of another leader of the breakaway group. Rusty razors, flick knives and coshes were used but, undaunted, the Cortesis regrouped. In November, just before midnight, Darby and Harry Sabini were drinking in the Fratellanza Club in Clerkenwell. The club was just a few doors from where the Cortesis lived. They moved onto the offensive, trapping the Sabinis in the club and attacking Darby with bottles. His brother Harry-Boy was not so lucky. He was shot but not seriously injured. Gangsters were normally very careful, when shooting, not to kill as they were likely to get a death sentence. The Cortesis were arrested that night and sentenced the following January at the Old Bailey to three years' penal servitude. Without leadership, the threat to the Sabini control disappeared. They were back in charge.

A less threatening figure regularly seen on the racecourse was Prince Monolulu. He was a tipster whose notoriety came about when he tipped the 1920 Derby winner Spion Kop at 100–6. He was a West Indian and, apart from Paul Robeson and Hutch, was probably the best known coloured man in Great Britain. His catchphrase 'I gotta horse', combined with his colourful jackets and feathered headdress, guaranteed he was often the centre of attention in the betting ring.

The jockeys and the horses

Whilst the extraordinary mix of the crowds, combined with the tipsters and bookies formed a colourful background for racing, the real stars were the jockeys and the horses they rode. National Hunt racing was now very much the poor relation to flat racing, which gained far more press coverage and interest. This was particularly true of the Classics. Whilst aristocratic owners were still represented, increasingly they were being joined by 'new money', financiers and manufacturers who had made fortunes during the war. It was a sport that had once been dominated by class but latterly by money. A few trainers were drawn from the gentry but for the most part they were either ex-jockeys or from families with a long tradition in racing. Because of this social divide a degree of subservience tended to pervade the sport. Jockeys were not only expected to perform well in the saddle, but to be respectful and diplomatic when dealing with owners. Few of them made a great living on fees of three guineas a ride and five guineas for a win. Jump jockeys were paid more, to take account of the additional dangers and injuries they were likely to sustain. Some jockeys tried to supplement their income by betting on what they felt was inside information. Unfortunately, jockeys had a reputation for being notoriously bad tipsters and many ran into severe financial difficulties due to their betting.

Nevertheless, in this burgeoning age of celebrity, two jockeys became household names.

Steve Donoghue and Humorist

Steve Donoghue became champion jockey in 1914. He retained the title for ten consecutive years. He won the Derby six times, twice at Newmarket during the war. His first Epsom Derby win was in 1921 on Humorist. He scored again with Captain Cuttle the following year and then again with Papyrus in 1923. Jockeys tend to be associated with certain horses, though they ride hundreds, possibly thousands, during the course of their careers. Donoghue is often linked to his Derby winner Humorist but for rather sad reasons. Steve had been criticised when he was beaten on the horse in the Two Thousand

Steve Donoghue on the ill-fated Humorist, winner of the 1921 Derby, painted by Alfred Munnings.

Guineas. Starting as favourite, Humorist appeared to have the race won but when Donoghue asked for a final effort the horse's stride shortened as they met the rising ground, eventually only finishing third. The jockey had noticed similar, though less pronounced, problems previously. Despite this, he was still convinced the horse could win the Derby. Donoghue was released by Lord Derby who normally retained his services to ride Humorist. During the race the jockey 'scraped the paint', running close to the inside rail, thereby taking the shortest course. Leaving his challenge late he urged the horse to go and win the race, which he did by a neck after an epic struggle with Eran. The horse was distressed after the race but was largely ignored in the euphoria surrounding his win. Later, still not himself, the horse was withdrawn from the Hardwicke Stakes. The artist Alfred Munnings was commissioned to paint the horse at Letcombe Regis by his owner, Mr Jim Joel. Having made a few sketches, Munnings enjoyed a good lunch with the horse's trainer, Charlie Morton, and went into the garden to sleep it off. When eventually he returned to the horse's stable he found Humorist lying dead covered in blood. A post-mortem revealed the horse had a long-standing tubercular lung condition. Amazingly, it was concluded that Humorist had won the Derby with only one functioning lung.

Most jockeys are superb horsemen but, as in all sports, occasionally someone comes along with that unexplained, additional skill. Donoghue fell into that category. He had the ability to bring out the best in a horse, a sixth sense that communicated itself to his mount. He was reckoned to be the best jockey since the legendary Fred Archer. Being an early superstar, Donoghue didn't have to survive on the slender pickings available to the average jockey. He was able to secure a number of lucrative retainers from leading owners anxious to secure his services. He was also paid a sizeable bonus for winning. It was reported that he received £2,000 from the owner of his Derby win on Humorist. Retainers could be as high as £5,000 and Donoghue had several of these at the height of his success. He was in so much demand that he would blithely break contracts if it suited him. He was living life to the full, being seen regularly in London's nightspots and frittering away huge sums on gambling sprees.

Gordon Richards

The other star jockey was the young Gordon Richards. Unlike Donoghue, Richards was a rather shy, thoughtful man. In contrast to many jockeys, he was also a natural lightweight and never had to resort to debilitating wasting. He rode his first winner as a seventeen-year-old in 1921 at Leicester. He became champion jockey in his first full year in 1928 with 118 winners. Illness robbed him of the chance to retain his title the following year, but from 1927 he dominated the British flat-racing scene becoming champion jockey a staggering twenty-six times.

The owners

Without wealthy owners, racing couldn't exist. Although traditionally associated with the aristocracy, ownership was increasingly being taken up by financiers, businessmen and the professions. National Hunt ownership, meanwhile, was still dominated by the squirearchy and wealthy farmers. The royal family retained an interest in racing, although George V was more interested in breeding than gambling. The top owners, like Lord Derby and the Aga Khan, employed racing managers on generous salaries of between £2,000 and £3,000 a year. The Aga Khan was reputed to spend an eye-watering £250,000 a year on his racing activities. He was rewarded by owning the greatest filly in training during the twenties. Mumtaz Mahal was named after the favourite wife of the emperor Shah Jahan, who was responsible for the building of the Taj Mahal. She was a beautiful grey, purchased for 9,000 guineas as a yearling, and earned her nickname of 'the flying filly'. She broke course records wherever she ran, some of which took generations to surpass.

Lord Rosebery's stud at Mentmore was one of the finest in the country and yet he was unable to fulfil his ambition of breeding a Derby winner there, although his son was successful, after his death, with Blue Peter and Ocean Swell. Lord Astor never won the Derby but was the leading owner in 1925 with winnings in excess of £35,000. Death duties and the general economic conditions restricted all but the super rich from owning top quality horses. The average price of about £800 for a yearling, plus training costs, precluded most. It was reckoned that to keep a horse in training cost as much as maintaining a mistress in the West End. There were over 4,600 horses in training in 1929. The figures for mistresses are not available!

Increasingly, foreign owners were becoming involved with British racing. Americans were prominent, as were a variety of fabulously wealthy maharajas. Of over 500 winning owners in 1926, 138 were either titled or had a senior military rank. Some of these owners were more interested in breeding lines, whilst others were gamblers. Mainly though, ownership was sought for the excitement. However, then as now, racing is ninety-five per cent disappointment and five per cent elation. If you are lucky, that is!

14

What's in Store?

'A bargain is something you can't use at a price you can't resist.'

(Franklin Jones)

Cranes and scaffolding dominate the skyline. It's 1923 and there is a building boom changing the face of much of the West End. Death duties and higher taxation has led not just to the selling of country estates, but also many of London's grandest houses. They are being replaced by massive new retail stores and picture palaces. The West End is becoming largely non-residential and the super rich are migrating to Mayfair, Knightsbridge and Kensington. Meanwhile, the burgeoning middle classes are setting up home in the leafy suburbs, now being serviced by the outreach of the underground system. It is to tempt these new and important customers that the stores are being built and refurbished.

Shopping was the one activity that all Londoners had in common. True, the grandest could leave the buying of everyday provisions to their butler or cook, but even the great and the good would occasionally go to a favoured store. Then, of course, regular visits were required to one's dressmaker, whilst the gentleman of the house made the odd trip to Savile Row. At the other end of the scale, street markets still flourished as they had done since the Middle Ages.

The rise and rise of the department store

The more fashionable independent shopkeepers in the West End were bemoaning the fact that their clientele appeared to be changing. They

A rare 1920s photograph of Peter Jones in Sloane Square.

reported that 'this new breed of ladies wanted the most up to date styles but for a very modest outlay'. The shopkeepers were being forced to cut their profit margins and sell up to five times the quantity of goods to make the same profit as previously. It was still the small shops that dominated in sheer numbers, but in central London they were under deadly attack. The new and expanding department stores were able to offer an enormous range of goods, often at prices the independent retailer couldn't match. Goods were not only drawn from traditional British manufacturers but from across the world, including the still mighty Empire.

In up-market Knightsbridge, Harrods had been established for many years, starting with a single room on the present site in 1851. The building we know today was completed in 1905 following a major fire a decade earlier. By the 1920s, Harrods had become one of the largest stores in the world, where it was reckoned you could purchase virtually anything. If the store didn't stock the item, no matter how bizarre, it would get it for you. Harrods also boasted the most comprehensive food hall, where it was possible to buy anything from a bag of sugar to a haunch of venison. It advertised in November 1926 '... Ever at your behest, either by personal inspection or by telephone instructions.' Harrods had become a national institution underlining its motto 'Everything for everybody'.

Harvey Nichols had also been in Knightsbridge since the nineteenth century, but was taken over by Debenhams in 1919. This early acquisition was to set a trend in the hyper-competitive retail trade. Down the road in Kensington the well-heeled residents were served by Barkers, and Derry and Toms. It was further to the east in Oxford Street and Regent Street that the real retail revolution was taking place. The redevelopment of Regent Street had been delayed by the war, but now there was a rush to create what promised to be London's premier retail thoroughfare.

Regent Street – a retail dream come true

The new Swan and Edgar store in Regent Street was typical of what was happening in retail development. Previously it had been housed in a number of ramshackle adjoining buildings, which failed to give

Advertisement for the opening of the iconic London store.

it a true identity. The new, modern store incorporated all of its departments under one roof. Some thought the building was trying to ape the mighty Selfridges or even Waring and Gillow further down Oxford Street. Certainly, its arrival indicated a general intensifying of competition with the stores resorting to sale promotions and personal appearances of well-known celebrities to boost trade. The entire Swan and Edgar store was built in less than two years, with the contractors regularly working through the night with the help of flares. The builders, Higgs and Hill, had created a reputation for completing contracts in good time and they were also responsible for other major buildings in Regent Street. As well as Aquascutum and Dickens & Jones, there was also the iconic Liberty building.

Liberty

Liberty had occupied a small shop on Regent Street selling mainly quirky antiques and other goods from Asia since 1875. Its founder, Arthur Lasenby, also championed the Arts and Crafts movement led by William Morris. He had a vision to create a unique style of store. Unfortunately, he died in 1917 and it was left to a Captain Liberty, no less, to create a totally English-looking store. He fought tenaciously with the Crown Commissioners to agree to what was, and still remains, one of the most controversial buildings in London. You either love it or hate it. Is it true to English heritage or just a shallow pastiche? It was constructed using the timbers from two old ships. The HMS *Hindustan* was completed back in 1814, whilst HMS *Impregnable* was launched some fifty-one years later. The latter had been the largest wooden ship afloat at the time. Amazing care was given to the shop detail with hand-made roof tiles and even the external leadwork fashioned in the traditional manner. The quality of the store's interior was also unrivalled with much of it being finished in Liberty's own workshops. For all the care and attention devoted to it, the building was certainly not greeted with uniform acclaim. It did, however, provide a perfect backdrop for Liberty's range including Eastern rugs, antiques, Clarice Cliff ceramics and Tudric pewterware.

* * *

177

Austin Reed had been in Regent Street since 1911 and its new store showed great innovation in its layout. Previously known mainly for the sale of shirts, Austin Reed's new building allowed the company to expand by offering a complete range of menswear. Each department was presented in a totally different type of setting. Made-to-measure suits were fitted in the grand and traditional setting of the Louis XV Room, whilst for those travelling abroad, tropical kit was displayed in a department decorated in red lacquer-work. The sporting and country clothes covered two floors with a Tudor decorative theme. It was left to the shoe department to offer the cutting edge of a truly Art Deco background.

Many stores trading back in the twenties remain on Regent Street today. Liberty, Aquascutum, Austin Reed and Hamleys, the famous toy store, are still thriving. However, almost all of the small shops have gone. They hung on for a few years selling corsetry, furs and championing other trades like watchmakers and jewellers whose goods had been associated with the area for many years. Even some of the stores that saw off these small traders have fallen away. Swan and Edgar, which had opened its new store to great acclaim in 1927, is no more. Another departmental store, Jay's, which occupied an important site on the south-east side of Oxford Circus, couldn't last the course. Originally known as a specialist in mourning-ware, it took years to throw off its funereal image by expanding into more artistic and mainstream ranges. (I had a very pompous uncle who was a director of the store until just after the end of the Second World War.) In a cryptic offering, H. T. Lyon wrote:

> *Now the aunt*
> *You deeply cherished*
> *Throughout long*
> *Declining years*
> *Leaves a legacy*
> *That will not*
> *Pay the mourning*
> *Bills at Jay's.*

The 1920s also witnessed the arrival of Galeries Lafayette to the east side of Regent Street. French chic was much in vogue, but their latest models were copied and produced in the sweatshops of Leeds and the East End. Stewarts Restaurant was a popular meeting place as diners looked down on the street already clogged with traffic whilst, nestled next to the Café Royal, the *Times* had a West End office. By 1927, the redevelopment of Regent Street was complete and the stores ready to compete with the brash American intruder, Gordon Selfridge. He had already greatly enlarged his huge, grand flagship store near Marble Arch on Oxford Street. The official opening of Regent Street was on 23rd June 1927. Although attended by the king and queen, it was a relatively modest affair, with only a few mounted servants and policemen following the royal couple. Although the king had requested that decorations and expensive lighting should be kept to a minimum (he was paying lip service to worsening trade conditions), there were still banks of flags and bunting to greet them. In addition, there were over 20,000 blooms including sweet peas, roses and geraniums, all in Queen Mary's favourite colours.

Unfortunately for the traders, business was already beginning to worsen. They were trapped in their smart, new premises, saddled with construction costs that had soared and ground rents demanded by the Crown Estates well above what most had budgeted for. They formed themselves into the Regent Street Association in an attempt to present a united front. Success in business is often all about timing and they were not to know that the Depression was just around the corner. Perhaps the General Strike the year before should have been a warning.

Selfridges

Meanwhile, down the road on Oxford Street, Selfridges was constantly raising the bar in the development of new and innovative retailing. What is it about short men that gives them that extra dynamism? Rejected by the US military for being too short, it was said that Harry Gordon Selfridge took to wearing Cuban heels. More importantly, he married into the wealthy Buckingham family. By 1906, Gordon Selfridge had already made a fortune by selling the American department store Schlesinger & Meyer. He sensed a tremendous opportunity to bring some of his American expertise to what he considered a dowdy, uninspired British market. Within two years he had invested a huge amount (estimated at £400,000) to open his store in the still under-developed Oxford Street, which was once overwhelmingly populated by small retailers, most of whom continued to live above their shops. His vision was that shopping should be an enjoyable experience, backed up by his famous motto: 'The customer is always right.' By the twenties, many of the Edwardian restrictions and conventions had been cast aside. Now it was acceptable for ladies to walk unaccompanied and he set out to appeal to this newly emancipated market.

The original store, which covered the area close to Duke Street, was extended to its present commanding size in 1923. Now Selfridge went into overdrive in an attempt to gain custom. No gimmick was too outlandish. A lifeboat from Ernest Shackleton's ship, *The Endurance*, was hoisted onto the store's roof. Shoppers were introduced to Suzanne Lenglen, Georges Carpentier and a host of other celebrities brought in to promote the store. In 1925, John Logie Baird gave the first public demonstration of a fledgling television. The following year, the first escalators were installed by the Otis Elevator Company. Selfridge was now suggesting that his customers should spend all day in the store. No expense was spared in the spectacular Palm Court restaurant or the stunning roof garden. Spiritualism had become popular following the war and leading exponents gave lectures in the restaurant. A mind-reading duo, the Zanzigs, entertained invited guests at the store on election night in 1921. The promotions and special events were never ending. How was the competition going to be able to rival this extraordinary, entrepreneurial showman? Well, a few hundred yards along the street, another household name was stirring. It was to offer a totally different philosophy, not so much in terms of retailing as such, but as a revolutionary approach to staff involvement.

John Lewis

The John Lewis ethos that all its staff were to be partners in the business had an extremely difficult birth. The original founder, John Lewis, belonged to the old school and he had a difficult relationship

180

Spedan Lewis, the instigator of the John Lewis Partnership ethos.

John Lewis, an uncompromising boss.

with his son, Spedan, whose ideas he viewed with alarm. They had a fundamental disagreement on how to run a business. Lewis senior was very set in his ways and autocratic in his approach. Matters came to a head in 1920, when the staff in his Oxford Street store went on strike. At the time, a sales assistant of twenty-one with three years experience was paid £2.15 a week. However, they had to pay over 10/- a week for their food and another 10/- for the staff hostel if they lived in. Lewis, together with other store owners, had agreed to increase wages as recommended by the Grocery Owners Board, but this was still considered to be too low for central London. In addition, staff wanted to be able to leave the store during their lunch break. The strike was scheduled to take place during a planned mammoth silk sale on 26th April. John Lewis had no intention of being browbeaten by his staff. He closed every other department, transferring the small number of employees not striking to the silk department. All the stock was sold by four o'clock that afternoon. The strike dragged on for weeks, but the crabby eighty-four-year-old had no intention of backing down. He issued a notice to 'our young men and maidens. What is it that gives rise to this unwholesome atmosphere? It is the vapourings of the accursed trade unionists.' He was later quoted as saying, referring to the strikers, 'If I see them on their hands and knees, I shall not take them back!' And he didn't. He won. There were other people prepared to fill the vacant posts. The strike fizzled out.

Meanwhile, his son Spedan Lewis had been running Peter Jones and it was 1924 before the two men settled their differences. It was two years later that Spedan acquired his brother's interest in the Oxford Street store. He wasted little time in instituting much of his enlightened management methods that had been in place at Peter Jones, including staff committees and claims for sick pay. On the trading front, the most obvious change was in the appointment of specialist window-dressers. His father had always allocated one window space for each buyer to display their wares, resulting in an unappealing hotchpotch. Spedan now had to compete with Selfridges with all their gimmicks and modern sales techniques.

It was only on John Lewis's death in 1928 that his son felt free to instigate his ideas about partnership that he had been planning for so

The silk department at John Lewis, pictured in 1930.

long. The John Lewis constitution was laid out for its partners in a hardbound book running to over 270 pages. It decreed codes of practice covering every conceivable situation. The scope was bewildering, including areas of dress, illness and absence and also, bizarrely, an instruction to partners not to bring firearms to work. Staff were instructed not to smoke during working hours because of the lingering smell on their breath and clothes. They were never to exit a lift before a customer. No customer was to be over-pressed to buy an item or scared off, no matter what the provocation. On a more prosaic level, no customer was to be contacted by telephone if writing would do just as well. Staff attendance was 8.55 a.m. to 6.10 p.m., Saturdays 8.55 a.m. to 1.10 p.m. The closing bell was to sound at six o'clock each evening and only then could goods start to be put away. Partners were given forty-five minutes for lunch, which was taken in their own dining-room. In addition, twenty minute tea breaks were allowed twice a day. Much of this was quite unlike terms offered to the staff of other retailers, although the senior staff were still deducted 8/9 per week for food and 1/8 for tea. The constitution warned that these charges did not include second helpings! Nothing was left to chance. Staff at Peter Jones were housed in a hostel above the store with the sexes strictly segregated. The ladies had a library provided whilst the men could spend their evenings playing billiards. The girls had to be in by nine o'clock and the men were allowed an hour extra.

The creation of the partnership and the profit-sharing scheme was big news and covered extensively in the national press. The idea seemed to fly in the face of normal business practice. It was criticised and derided in many quarters. This was surely setting an extremely dangerous precedent.

The new partners at John Lewis had barely come to grips with their improved situation when the company effectively doubled in size with the acquisition of T. J. Harries further along Oxford Street. Again, this store was housed in a ramshackle assortment of old buildings, but had the advantage of having a much greater frontage on to Oxford Street. Much of the new purchase was given over to fashion and accessories, which, due to lack of space, had previously been tucked away in the recesses of John Lewis. The store's main emphasis had always been on furniture, home furnishings and piece goods. Now, with the two outlets, John Lewis was able to separate the stock so that all the ranges could be displayed effectively. The new group was now able to proudly proclaim the motto used previously at Peter Jones, and that still remains today: 'Never knowingly undersold.'

So the battle lines were drawn in the West End for the consumer's cash. Service was everything and at a level we would wonder at today. Long mahogany counters staffed by assistants every few feet. Even the smallest item was carefully wrapped in tissue paper. Think of shopping without computers or even, in most cases, cash registers. Every purchase carefully recorded by hand. The customer sitting on a chair by the counter, whilst the assistant went to the cashier to get the change. Always a personal service in an atmosphere of calm, quite unlike today's shopping experience.

Of course, not all department stores were situated in the West End. Jones Brothers in Holloway Road supplied a huge range of products aimed at a lower section of the market. Probably the best known store outside the West End was Gamages in Holborn. Like all the other stores, except Selfridges, it had a very humble beginning, trading from one scruffy room. But these early retailers were prepared to make huge sacrifices to get their businesses started. From the beginning, Gamages set out to be the cheapest for whatever it sold. The store expanded through a maze of rooms and corridors to become known as 'The People's Popular Emporium'. By the 1920s it ran a huge range with sporting and camping equipment being a speciality. It also had one of the largest toy departments in the country, usually selling at bargain prices. It had also acquired the rights to become the official supplier of Boy Scout uniforms, in a period when scouting was at its height.

Marks & Spencer

Whilst Gamages based its attraction simply on price, another organisation, who is still with us today, was looking far deeper into consumer needs. Marks & Spencer can trace its origins back to a Leeds market stall in the 1880s. Until the outbreak of the Great War, it had remained essentially a northern group of penny bazaars, although a few branches had ventured into Greater London.

It was American influence and expertise that inspired Simon Marks to guide the company in a new direction. He had watched the US Woolworth chain grow and gain a rapid foothold in the British market. Unlike the giant department stores which relied largely on the aspirational buying power of the middle classes, Woolworth offered its entire range for 6d or less. A sure case that if you look after the pennies the pounds look after themselves. Woolworth offered good quality products with acres of counters for display.

In 1924, Marks set off for the States on a fact-finding tour. He came back inspired, with a vision of how to change not only the company, but also how to alter the face of British retailing. The penny bazaars were swiftly converted into a chain of superstores. By 1928, the famous green and gold logo and fascia had been introduced together with the comforting St Michael brand name. These were the obvious outward signs of change, but away from the public gaze far more fundamental changes were being instigated. Whilst other retailers had been dealing direct with manufacturers, thus cutting out the traditional middle man, Marks & Spencer took the link an important step further. It was the first British retailer to work with manufacturers to mass produce exclusive products for its own stores. The organisation co-operated on design, quality and forward projections on likely sales. It adopted US stock control systems, which tied manufacturers to its requirements. Its methods were particularly successful regarding its rapid expansion into the area of affordable women's fashions. By the end of the decade, M&S was able to introduce ranges of good quality dresses all to sell for under five shillings, the price limit that had been set for all goods in its stores. It also accepted returned goods for a full cash refund. This combination was irresistible. By 1930, Marks & Spencer had arrived in Oxford Street to increase West End competition still further.

Sainsbury's

Meanwhile, Sainsbury's was already the largest grocer in the country. Many of its shops were laid out with marble-topped counters, behind which immaculately dressed assistants stood anxious to help. They wore uniforms topped by crisp, white aprons. The bacon departments alone employed several staff, whilst butter and cheese was cut to order. The abiding memory was of smell. The wonderful aroma of coffee and tea competing with dried bacon. The coffee was ground and blended to each customer's requirements. There was relatively little pre-packaged food. Most items had to be weighed and wrapped. There was a huge selection of teas available, many of which had to be measured from wooden chests. There was a ritual and skill in the way each commodity was prepared, whilst the customer sat at the counter on a high-backed chair, chatting to the assistant.

So London had become a Mecca for shopping, whatever your circumstances. The street markets thrived, although the police were constantly trying to close down the famous Petticoat Lane as it was largely unregulated. Like most of the other street markets, it had a reputation for handling stolen goods. On both sides of the river the markets provided an atmosphere of noise and colour. In Berwick Street you were able to buy all sorts of exotic fruit and vegetables only normally seen in Harrods food hall. The 1920s was key in dragging British retailing away from its Edwardian comfort zone. The modern world had arrived, requiring hard work, flair and efficiency. There had to be an understanding of what the public needed and desired in a rapidly changing world. Only the best would survive.

15

Selling the Suburban Dream

'Suburbia is where the developer bulldozes out the trees, then names the streets after them.'

(Bill Vaughan)

Traffic jams are not a modern phenomenon. By the beginning of the 1920s, the streets of central London had become clogged and chaotic. For the most part the roads of the ancient capital were quite unsuited to the snarling mass of cars and lumbering buses belching exhaust fumes. In amongst the mêlée there were a few remaining horse-drawn carts, but their days were numbered. This was the decade when public transport would assert itself. Londoners would be taken not only to their place of work, but were offered new opportunities for transporting them to sporting venues, cinemas and even weekend trips to the countryside.

As thousands of troops returned from the war, London's transport system was at breaking point. Huge additional numbers of buses and trams were required. For a time, buses that had been used for the troops were brought into service. Some were still painted khaki with uncomfortable wooden slatted seats and the upper deck open to the elements, or possibly covered with a rough tarpaulin. Trams were excluded from the up-market areas of Westminster and the City. They were considered to be more suitable for the working classes. Even on the outskirts of town the authorities insisted that there should be no unsightly wires or poles necessitating the installation of an expensive conduit system. Luckily, the Underground was functioning well, and in 1920 new cars were brought into service on the Piccadilly line incorporating air-operated doors. Still, the trams were immensely important, carrying over 70 million passengers per year across some 1,100 miles of tramways.

189

A busy Oxford Circus with crowds flocking to the shops. The age of consumerism is already in full swing.

Gotta get some wheels – the car and the city

Meanwhile, the aspiring classes were peering enviously into the car showrooms of Piccadilly. By 1920 the Automobile Association was boasting a membership of a hundred thousand. In 1922 the well-known racing driver Jack Barclay formed a partnership trading as Barclay and Wyse selling the rather strange combination of Rolls-Royce and Vauxhall cars. By 1927 their success was underlined by the establishment of a prestigious headquarters in Hanover Square.

A motor car was now top of the wish-list for every aspiring Londoner.

People from the professions and senior commercial managers were now in a position to buy cars. A bewildering array of manufacturers set up in an attempt to satisfy demand. Whilst some had already been established before the war, most are now forgotten, like Crouch Cars, manufactured in Coventry until 1928. Better known names also perished over the years – the Jowett, Swift and the up-market Armstrong Siddeley, together with dozens of other similar marques. For the most part, volume was the key to success and the market was led by Morris with its popular bull-nosed model. Austin and Ford were not far behind in supplying affordable cars. Driving in London was stressful, but so was life generally. Rush and hustle suited some, but many sought a more peaceful existence, at least at home. New swathes of arterial roads were being laid, allowing the Western Avenue, the Great Western Road and the North Circular to attract modern factories and employment. Houses were built on green field sites to accommodate staff. The Golden Mile, as it was known, was opened by the king in 1925. The factories were producing an array of goods, including radios, cycles, toothpaste and Smith's crisps.

Metroland and the birth of suburbia

The extension of the Underground network and the continuing thrust of the Metropolitan Railway towards the Chilterns led to an explosion of house building in London suburbs and Metroland. The poet John Betjeman, whilst understanding Londoners' aspirations to own a house in a leafy suburb, had his reservations. Famously, he wrote, 'Come friendly bombs and fall on Slough, it isn't fit for humans now.' He did, however, soften his views slightly when he stated, 'People's backyards are much more interesting than their front gardens and houses that back onto railways are public benefactors.'

Metroland had come into modern parlance as early as 1915. It covered a roughly defined area north of Wembley and on to the Chilterns, which was covered by the Metropolitan Railway. The company's directors had understood the potential for colonising existing villages and hamlets, by building stations providing a regular service to central London and the City. The railway company set up an

Ticket machines were already in use on the London Underground by 1928.

arms-length subsidiary called Metropolitan Country Estates. Whilst the Metropolitan Railway itself was forced to give up direct association with the new subsidiary, it continued to work closely with its offshoot, nominating the Estate's chairman and other directors. It also provided a prestigious head office in Baker Street. A Metroland magazine priced tuppence was produced, which advertised the advantages of living out of town, yet within easy reach by train. Advertising was also placed in the *Railway Magazine*, extolling the virtues of 'being able to travel to and from the City without change of carriage, whilst Baker Street is linked by escalator with the underground electric system. So there is every facility for expeditiously reaching any part of London'. Semi-detached houses with three bedrooms were being offered for £1,200 in 1920, which was considered expensive. The company was also targeting first class passengers, with four-bedroomed houses on the Cedars Estate in Rickmansworth with half-acre plots for £2,250.

The attractions of a semi-rural life included the impressive leisure facilities on offer. In addition to tennis clubs, Metroland boasted over a dozen eighteen-hole golf courses 'amidst picturesque hills, dales and woods and promising every charm that the lover of sport and invigorating air can possibly desire!' Whilst sophisticated Londoners sneered at the bourgeois appeal of the suburbs, the rapidly expanding estates sold quickly. The attraction was proving irresistible. Whilst the husband was at work, his wife could take the train to Baker Street for a little shopping in the West End. She could even meet up with her husband after work and have supper at the conveniently situated Chiltern Court Restaurant above Baker Street station. It promised perfect cuisine and faultless service. Unfortunately, it never made money as its rather grand colonaded décor was considered outdated.

By 1922 private builders were in full flood, taking over from public authorities who had suffered a reduction in government subsidies. This suited the railway company because local authority housing tended to be rented accommodation and occupants seldom used the railway. Development east of Harrow was accelerated, with stations being built at Northwick Park and Kenton. Houses sprang up in Eastcote and Ickenham, but proved harder to sell in Pinner, which, although attractively situated, required a two-mile walk to the nearest station. Still, advertisements pressed home the advantages of country houses in Metroland. Properties on the upmarket Rickmansworth estate with plots of over an acre were snapped up at prices in excess of £3,000.

The Empire Exhibition of 1924 offered a fresh opportunity for trumpeting the delights of Metroland to the hordes of visitors. The expansion accelerated. Viscount Leverhulme purchased a 3,000-acre estate between Northwood and Rickmansworth, before selling it on to Moor Park Ltd. The company developed two superb golf courses and an extremely up-market housing estate.

The Moor Park and Sandy station was to prove a lucrative source of income for the railway. By 1925 the line had been electrified leading to further development in Croxley Green and Watford. Part-time Londoners were becoming a fast growing tribe, commuting to town each morning, before returning to their mock Elizabethan villas in mock semi-rural splendour at night. As yet most areas were not overdeveloped. Residents were often able to look out over open countryside. But for how long? There was money to be made. More houses were already being squeezed in per acre. For some the dream was beginning to fade, but the builders and estate agents didn't let this dampen their enthusiasm. An advertisement for houses being constructed just outside Watford read '... noticeable for its abundance of charming features and no more delectable spot could be desired as a place of residence. It is undulating in character, possesses a subsoil of gravel, sand and chalk, is commandingly situated near Rickmansworth station and extends from this old world country town westward over hill, dale and woodland to Chorley Wood's breezy common, where it is flanked by trim plantation that provide a perfect feast for the eye.' Today, those same houses are surrounded by legions of rooftops and gardens concreted for parking cars and caravans.

Other advertisements were asking potential buyers whether they were going to be satisfied with mass-produced houses, with sham half-timbering? Or, were they seeking a house of distinction created by qualified architects and true craftsmen? Most were opting for the mass-produced version, which was affordable, with semis now available for as little as £700 freehold, or at a rental of £90 per year. The onward march of new housing was unstoppable – Wealdstone, Hatch End, Kingsbury all surrendered to street upon street of mock Elizabethan villas. Not for the English the modernist architecture favoured by much of continental Europe. Londoners colonising the suburbs felt comfortable with mini versions of how they imagined 'the toffs' lived, although *their* properties were usually hidden from the public's gaze along tree-lined drives. The new dwellers occupied their own mini castles and mansions, sheltered from their neighbours' gaze only by net curtains. In Middlesex, by the end of the decade the advantages of semi-rural living had largely disappeared under a sea of rooftops. Expansion into Buckinghamshire had stalled and it was reckoned that Metroland had Great Missenden as its furthest outpost; the problem being that the train journey to London took the best part of an hour.

The London County Council, meanwhile, was building eight cottage estates, which were initially labelled as 'fit for heroes'. Beacontree Estate, between Barking and Dagenham, was the largest in the world, providing houses for many of the Ford workers employed at the Dagenham plant. The estate was also an attempt by the authorities at slum clearance from the blackest spots in the East End. Many of those moving to the estate were unhappy in their new surroundings, complaining about the time and cost of getting to work. Most of all, they missed the closeness of the deprived community they had left behind. Another group of East Enders were leaving due to their success. Flourishing Jewish traders were migrating to Dalston and Stoke Newington, with a few setting up an outpost in Golders Green, where the Dunstan Road synagogue was opened in 1922.

The Underground, Frank Pick and London Transport

In addition to the Metropolitan Railway, it was the Underground that contributed most to the expansion of the suburbs. The network had started at the end of the nineteenth century with the line connecting Stockwell to the City of London. By 1920, the London Electric Railway Company ran the tube system. Frank Pick, a trained lawyer, had by now taken up the post of publicity manager. He was to be as influential for the London transport system as John Reith was in radio. Like Reith he had been brought up with strong Christian beliefs and an unstinting work ethic. He not only had an eye for enduring design, but also the foresight to commission the most talented artists to interpret his ideas. The bullseye trademark for the Underground and buses is still used today. The symbol has become synonymous with London transport. Like all classic logos, it has stood the test of time, being simple, yet striking and memorable. Pick set out to encourage Londoners not to use the tube purely for going to and from work. He needed them to use the trains for visiting sporting events and a whole range of leisure activities. Posters were created advertising museums and places of public interest, and encouraging travel at off-peak times. Leading artists, such as Frank Brangwyn, had begun to appreciate the kudos of having their work displayed across the platforms and booking halls of the network. Neither did Pick shy away from commissioning cutting edge artists from the modern schools of Cubism and Vorticism. This had the effect of promoting the Underground as a modern and efficient means of transport. Pick was a detail man. He even employed Edward Johnston, a leading calligraphist, to produce a standardised lettering for the posters so that a distinctive format was maintained.

Pick's influence reached far further than just visual design. In 1922, automatic doors were widely introduced as was attractive, standardised upholstery. That same year the Euston to Moorgate section of the Underground was closed so that the tunnels could be enlarged. In 1924, a service linking Camden Town to Highgate and Hendon was introduced. This, in turn, was extended to the network's northern outpost of Edgware. Speculative building followed along these new routes. Further sections were opened up from Moorgate to Clapham Common and onwards. By 1924, it was possible to travel from Edgware in the north to the southern outpost of Morden. So it was that places which for centuries had been little more than hamlets gave themselves up to an orgy of house building. The shape and character of Greater London was extending and changing on an almost daily basis.

By 1928, Frank Pick was appointed joint managing director of the organisation shortly to be known as 'London Transport'. Future prospects excited him. He appointed the architect Charles Holden, who was commissioned to design new stations on the southern extension of the Northern line. The group was now employing thousands of staff. Pick wanted a headquarters building that reflected the importance of the company for the people of London. Initial plans were rejected and Pick turned to Holden to produce one of London's iconic buildings, known simply as 55 Broadway. Four of the ten storeys were located in the tower and it was the nearest building to a skyscraper that London could boast. Pick had, undoubtedly, been influenced by a trip he had made to America. It was constructed of Portland stone fixed to a steel framework. The very plainness of the exterior was contrasted by the sculptures he commissioned for each side of the building. Works by Eric Gill, Henry Moore and particularly Jacob Epstein caused controversy and outrage. For a time it appeared that Pick might have to resign over his brave choice of modern sculptors. It was Epstein's figure 'Day' that most offended public taste. The giant figure of a naked man faces east towards the rising sun. It was rumoured that Epstein was asked to remove several inches of the carving's penis to calm matters. In any event, the spat subsided, helped no doubt by the building being awarded the London Architectural Medal by the Royal Institute of Architects. It remains one of London's major buildings of the period.

Frank Pick was a hardworking perfectionist, who took an interest in every aspect of the transport system that has served London so well. He designed rolling stock for the Northern line and even worried about the angle of the arm rests to ensure his passengers were as comfortable as possible. Nothing escaped his attention, from the fabrics for seating to the design of bus shelters. His influence had now extended to bus and tram services. He was responsible for the largest city transport authority in the world.

On Sundays and bank holidays families queued for buses, which still ran on solid tyres, to take them to the country, to beauty spots like Box Hill or Chislehurst. A whole new world was being opened up for Londoners. During the weekday rush hour, crowds caught buses, trams and trains to their homes in outer London. Change was everywhere. Former slum areas showed signs of being transformed. Areas on the outskirts had become suburbanised. Although times were still very tough for most, now at least there was hope. It was possible to escape the drudgery of everyday life as never before with a visit to a cinema or music hall. Mobility, even on public transport, was life changing. Looking down from the upper deck of the famous red buses at the few sports cars and chauffeur driven limousines, people were able to dream of a better life ahead.

Peter Jones fashions for autumn.

16

Changing Fashions

'Fashion is a form of ugliness so intolerable that we have to alter it every six months.'

(Oscar Wilde)

She sits at the bar. A waif, a boy-like figure with her hair shorn. In one hand she clasps a cigarette holder, so long that the cigarette itself is almost lost in the smoke ring she blows. In the other hand is her powder compact. She gazes into its mirror, checking her bright red lipstick. Why did women want to look like young men in the 1920s? Theories abound. Many had undertaken men's work during the war. They had cut their hair short to work in factories or on the land. Fashion historian, James Laver, suggested that far from wanting to appear masculine, women were out to look sexier. Bosoms were associated with motherhood; they had to go. So did corsets. It was time for a revolution, in fashion at least! A contemporary commentator quoted by Laver states, 'The angular English woman, over whose lack of *embonpoint* papers like *La Vie Parisienne* have been making merry for two generations, has now become the accepted type of beauty!'

Women's fashion – birth of the flapper

A relatively slow-burning revolution at first. In 1920 skirts were still long, but already there was a tendency to camouflage the female curves so admired by the Edwardians. Waistlines disappeared along with long hair scrunched into buns. The appearance of the cloche hat defined hairstyles throughout the decade. If the hair was not cut short it was not possible to wear the cloche. Only those with no interest in fashion defied the trend. Some women had worn their hair short before the war, but only the arty, bohemian set. Short hair had also been associated with free love and, worse, those ghastly Bolsheviks. Edwardian matriarchs shuddered at the way life was heading, but there was worse to come. By 1925 skirt lengths had been raised to go with the cropped hair. *Punch* ran a cartoon in which a young man is instructed 'grow your hair man, you look like a girl!' A year previously had seen the introduction of the bob, followed by the shingle and then, confusingly, a combination of the two, the bingle. There was a boom in the sales of methylated spirit stoves together with tongs, which enabled girls with straight hair to give themselves permanent waves. Few could afford the four guineas charged by Harrods to achieve the same effect. Still, fashion dictated that most hairstyles were still too long and 1927 saw the arrival of the Eton crop. With a totally flattened bust, it really was difficult now to distinguish a young woman from a schoolboy. Well, not entirely. The modern girl was likely to have reddened Cupid lips, pencilled eyebrows and the statutory look of utter boredom.

Cecil Beaton described the young women of the mid twenties as 'larger than life' with their 'short tubular dresses, cigarettes in long holders, cloche hats, bobbed hair, plucked eyebrows, bands of diamond bracelets from wrist to elbow and earrings hanging like fuschias.' He was presumably referring to well-to-do 'Bright Young Things', but the relative simplicity of popular fashions allowed ordinary girls to run up passable flapper dresses using their sewing machines and Butterick patterns. Whilst the young rejoiced in the freedom and skimpiness of the new fashions, the fabric manufacturers longed for a return to ankle-length dresses. They still had some time to wait. The new fashion was also a disaster for the corset manufacturers, with sales during the decade declining by two-thirds. They reacted swiftly by introducing the *bandeau*. This was pulled over the head and consisted of a rigid front band of cloth or lace. This was sufficient to cover the bust and was joined to a band of soft, ventilated cotton elastic. Stitched to the top edge were two non-adjustable shoulder straps. This had the effect of flattening the breasts, yet was comfortable to wear. Deep, flat-fronted bras were introduced. Sales were enormous and the bust bodice, which had flourished since the turn of the century, was left for the elderly. Symington, the leading British manufacturer, also introduced their side lacer, which also produced the desired flat look. Another popular innovation was the suspender girdle. Underwear now had to be light, comfortable and easy to wear. Camiknickers became all the rage as did camibockers, generally available in Japanese silk and crêpe de Chine, usually in a rather unappealing pink. By 1929 a new trio of bra, petticoat and knickers were in vogue.

Chanel and Schiaparelli

The Paris fashion houses also found themselves wrong-footed by the new trends. Several, including Doucet and Drecoll, were unable to adapt and were forced to close. Two new names came through to dominate and revolutionise the fashion trade. Coco Chanel came to represent everything the modern girl was looking for. Her clothes were designed for living in rather than just being seen in. They were for the modern girl. Someone who walked to work, climbed into cars and upstairs on London's buses. Chanel tended to favour neutral tones. Beige was very much the colour of the twenties. She was also fond of cream and sand, alternated with navy and black, in workable jersey fabrics. She was a good-looking woman, who mixed in artistic circles, becoming very close to Stravinsky, Cocteau and Picasso. In 1925 she introduced her cardigan jacket, but it is the ubiquitous little black dress with which she will always be associated. Her designs varied only slightly from season to season. Just enough to encourage further purchases, but giving an opportunity for a relatively prolonged stay in many a wardrobe.

Her main rival in influencing popular fashion in the high street was the Italian designer Elsa Schiaparelli. Her collections were more flamboyant and representative of the Art Deco age. Her designs shocked, thrilled and scandalised in equal measure. She was accused of bringing 'Apache' into the Ritz. She produced stylish, well-designed, relatively affordable clothes. Schiaparelli never learnt to sew. She set out a format by drawing her ideas on paper and getting her seamstresses to translate them. She was one of the first to market her collection

Coco Chanel, photographed in 1926.

by well-produced and elaborate fashion shows. She often created collections on a single theme. Her success was said to have rankled with Coco Chanel and yet their designs were so different. Chanel confined herself largely to the conservative, Schiaparelli to the outrageous. Both, in their way, were instrumental in bringing top quality fashion to a larger audience.

Bare arms were an ongoing feature of twenties fashion. This applied to both day and evening wear. Legs that had hardly been seen during the Edwardian era also took a bow. Thick black stockings and lace-up boots were out. Flesh-coloured stockings became the rage. They came in silk or rayon, often referred to as art silk. The downside with rayon was that it made the legs look shiny. The trick was to powder your legs before pulling up your stockings. The really fashion conscious girls sported stockings with patterns, which drew attention to a slim ankle and a shapely calf. In the winter, the girls were forced to cover up. A feature of coats during the twenties was the wrap-over style. This had just one side fastening and many featured shawls with fur collars. Peter Jones advertised 'a coat of black faced cloth from our own workrooms. The long roll collar and flounce of soft fur are very successful. It is lined with crêpe de Chine.' All this for just eleven guineas. Sensible tweeds were available for the sporty lady. Harrods advertised 'the call of the moors' in 1928 with smart double-breasted jackets and skirt lengths which had retreated to just below the knee.

The cloche hat, originally appealing to the young, now swept all before it as matrons besieged the hair salons. It was only possible to wear the cloche if the hair was cut really short. Most hats had brims that almost covered the eyes. Foreheads disappeared and the millinery trade enjoyed boom years. A collection of Marie Alphonsine millinery, described as being made of 'sparkling nacré remaille', sold at Harrods. The store also offered cloches in featherweight felt at 21/9 from its first-floor millinery department. This was still too expensive for most, but a trip to Jones Bros. in Holloway Road offered cloches made from a combination of velveteen and silk, complete with a flower

Evening chic personified.

1920s autumn fashion.

motif, for an amazing 4/11. For 9/11 they advertised felt hats, seemingly indistinguishable from the more expensive Harrods version. The most expensive hats on offer to the ladies of Holloway Road were made from Austrian velour and priced at 29/9. Meanwhile, at Peter Jones in Sloane Square, the ladies of substance were turning their thoughts to their servants. A maid's uniform in alpaca was available in a wide range of colours, complete with a Peter Pan collar and white apron for 27/9. For heavier work, the girl could be kitted out with Hercules overalls for 7/11, whilst parlour maids' caps were just 4/6. When madam took to her bed, Peter Jones was not about to supply nightwear that would arouse her husband too much after a busy day. Sensible pyjamas were available at 11/9, or passion crushing nightdresses at 14/11.

Taking an annual holiday was by now quite commonplace. Again, it was the young that shocked with their choice of swimwear. For most, bathing suits continued to preserve a lady's modesty, with two-piece costumes where the knickers stretched to the knees. The young opted for one-piece skin tight costumes, which left little to the imagination. The floppy mob caps were being replaced by tight-fitting elastic caps. Sunbathing was just beginning to be respectable, but most still thought that dark skin indicated you worked out of doors and was rather common. So even the young sheltered under parasols to protect their typically English complexions. Of course, by the thirties a suntan suddenly indicated wealth and an ability to avoid the filthy English summers by relaxing on the beaches of the Riviera.

The sweet smell of success – Arden and Rubinstein

Smoking in public was no longer frowned upon, nor was a girl fixing her make-up. It was estimated that each young woman owned several powder compacts. There were hundreds of face creams and a bewildering range of perfumes on sale. One famous brand exists to this day. Chanel No. 5 provided Coco Chanel with much of the profit she required to expand her fashion business. The overall cosmetic trade was dominated by two overpowering figures who produced the first brands to establish global penetration. Elizabeth Arden and Helena Rubinstein had so much in common and yet they never met. Arden, who was Canadian, with the help of a friend Fabian Swanson (a chemist), created her first 'beauty cream'. On a trip to Europe, Arden realised the potential of make-up, which had previously largely been the preserve of actresses or ladies of ill-repute. She set out with her husband, Thomas Lewis, to make cosmetics not just acceptable but desirable. The profit margins both for retailer and manufacturer were huge and soon stores were giving over their prime space to the cosmetic department. Arden introduced the use of beauty stylists in stores. Elizabeth never allocated or offered her husband any shares in the business. This obviously ate away at him until the marriage finally floundered in 1935, the same year she introduced her first perfume, Blue Grass. In a strange twist of fate, Thomas went to work for her arch rival Helena Rubinstein.

Rubinstein was already well established by the beginning of the decade. She also teamed up with a chemist so that her products were soundly based. Jacob Lykosky was a Hungarian whose formulation of facial cream produced the launching pad for the Rubinstein empire. Helena was tiny. Although standing at under five feet, she was a powerhouse, whose energy was combined with a considerable intellect. Born in Poland, she became an American citizen after stays in Australia and London, where she refined her business ambitions. Her range expanded to include face powders, rouge and lipsticks. She was interested in understanding the effects of diet on health and skincare. In 1928 she decided to concentrate on her European business, selling her American arm for over $7 million. Her timing was exquisite, coming just months before the crash. She paid only just over $1 million to buy the company back from Lehman Brothers.

The beauty business was in full flow and offering staggering profits. Cosmetic surgery became available for the first time. Ladies went for facials and young girls trained as beauticians. Hairdressing and beauty salons peppered the streets of London. Vanity reigned. Appearance became a priority for women of all ages. A mammoth industry was given free rein and it never looked back.

Men's fashion

Men were not about to be left behind. Patched elbows and pockets bulging with pens and pipes were still commonplace but, heaven help us, some men were actually becoming fashion conscious! Film stars were to blame. Young men started to ape the look they saw on the silver screen.

A prince of fashion

Another major trendsetter was the young Prince of Wales. Small in stature, but good-looking, he was seldom out of the papers. Brought up in the typically strict royal tradition, he showed a more approachable human style, which appealed to the British public. He was neither stuffy nor buttoned up. His father, sensing the loose cannon he had sired, said, 'After I'm dead the boy will ruin himself in twelve months.' His choice of friends tended to be on the louche side. He had a love of nightlife. Any club or restaurant he visited instantly became 'a must' to visit. With too much time on his hands, and with no intellectual pretensions, he devoted his life to enjoyment, when not being sent on official overseas tours. His interest in clothes propelled him as an unofficial ambassador for the young. He was pictured in Fair-Isle jumpers. The stores couldn't keep up with the demand. He wore Oxford bags. Every young man aspired to owning a pair. He tied his tie in what became known as the Windsor knot (which my own father likened to holding your knife and fork incorrectly). Suits were still the mainstay of middle Britain. An 'off-the-peg' suit could be purchased from the fifty-shilling tailors for under £2, whilst a bespoke version could be had for under £8. The Prince of Wales was seen sporting a chalk-striped, double-breasted suit in 1929.

The double-breasted dinner jacket had already gained in popularity after it was worn by Jack Buchanan in *Toni* at the Shaftesbury Theatre five years earlier. Now the style had been endorsed by the Prince of Wales, single-breasted suits with double-breasted waistcoats were deemed old-fashioned. Meanwhile, Harrods was offering a new spring overcoat in a range of interesting tweeds or plain and fancy covert cloths, available in single- or double-breasted, close-fitting styles, at six guineas. Still, most men wore hats. The cloth cap, very much associated with the working man, was also worn by middle-class golfers or farmers on market day. The top hat had fallen from favour except in the City, where now the bowler was the most popular form of headwear.

Apart from bankers, top hats were reserved for Royal Ascot and weddings. A young man turning up for interview for any white-collared job had to wear a hat to stand any chance. A smart trilby preferably, or possibly a pork pie. Boaters, much loved by public schools, were still seen on warm summer afternoons.

The clothes you wore defined who and what you were in life. There were strict rules that had to be honoured if you wanted to be acknowledged in class-ridden England. Shirt cuffs should always show just below the jacket sleeve. Only one button should be secured on a single-breasted jacket. Starched, rather than soft collars were essential for work. Two-tone shoes were considered to be only suitable for piano players in night-clubs. Suede shoes were reckoned to show homosexual leanings. If you wore grey shoes, frankly you were thought to be beyond the pale. The unwritten rules were prescriptive and not open to debate. Wearing brown shoes with a blue or grey suit would have people scurrying to avoid you. It was possible to play safe with a visit to John Lewis, which offered a range of shoes; and if the soles wore thin within three months they would be repaired free of charge and all for 30/-. A black patent leather shoe for evening wear, which still looks stylish today, cost 21/-. Trousers, even Oxford bags, had to have knife-edged creases. Cigarette cases were designed to be slim so as not to create unsightly bulges. Everyone smoked, but it was considered bad form to offer 'a gasper' from a packet. Cases were preferably gold or silver, although a pigskin version would just about pass muster. It was usual to house Virginia on one side of the case and Turkish on the other. Like their female counterparts, men were now even taking an interest in their hairstyle. It was fashionable to have it slicked back and covered in Brylcreem, or some expensive cologne, and parted down the middle.

So there they sit, our young twenties couple. The fashionable flapper girl with her svelte figure, short skirt and a string of pearls draped round her neck. At regular intervals she opens her handbag and applies another cloud of powder. Her companion, short and dapper, cigarette in his mouth, cocktail glass in hand. They talk in clipped accents that sound so affected to us today. But, has so much changed? London has changed, circumstances, too, but people remain very much the same. If it were possible to transfer our fictional couple to modern-day London it is pretty certain that within days they would find their feet and fit in. As would a young couple of today taken back to the twenties. The world evolves, London continues head down, rushing towards the future and the inhabitants take it all in their stride.

17

A Difficult Decade

'All people are most credulous when they are happy.'

(Walter Bagehot)

The fun had by Londoners in the 1920s was in spite of, rather than because of, the momentous happenings that formed a backdrop to their lives. There are some striking similarities with life today as the country continues to stagger from one crisis to another. Then, as now, governments overspent. There were dodgy politicians, cash for honours scandals, coalitions and industrial unrest. The British are a resilient lot and, in spite of hardship and unemployment, where possible they have always sought to relegate nagging problems to the back of their minds by going to a football match or seeking the escapism of the silver screen.

The end of the war saw a real threat of social breakdown. In London there were strikes on the Underground and by ship workers. Rent control during the war had led to landlords allowing their properties to fall into disrepair, and residential building had ground to a halt. Where were the droves of returning servicemen to live?

The real danger of a post-war slump led to Britain coming off the Gold Standard in an attempt to remain competitive in world markets. This fuelled a temporary speculative boom in London's property market. Money was loaned by the banks with an almost reckless abandon. Investors convinced themselves that there was easy money to be made (does this ring any bells?). Greed remains a constant across the generations.

The prime minister, Lloyd George, was a larger-than-life figure, with the appearance of an extrovert, theatrical impresario. He was

213

charismatic and personally charming with a gift for oratory. He was in favour of a continued reflation of the economy, which was viewed with increasing alarm by the Tories. The spring of 1920 saw growth on the continent smashed and the domestic boom going into a rapid reverse. Thousands of workers were laid off as higher interest rates led to a contraction in exports. By 1921 over two million were unemployed.

Tellingly, underlining Britain's reputation for suspicion of outsiders, London County Council banned foreigners from a wide range of council jobs. Many were to have been centred on County Hall, the council's impressive new headquarters, south of the river facing the Houses of Parliament.

There were continuing problems in Ireland, whilst suffragettes continued to make the news with Sylvia Pankhurst being jailed for six months for inciting London dockers to loot the docks. Women over thirty had gained voting rights in 1918, but it was another ten years before they were put on an equal footing with men.

In a forerunner to the General Strike of 1926, a miners' strike dominated the news early in 1921. During the war the mines had gone under public ownership, but a royal commission recommended an increase in miners' pay and permanent nationalisation of the pits. The government agreed to the pay increase but would not accept public ownership. Worried about the profitability of the mines with the collapse of the export market, the government returned the mines to their reviled owners in 1921. The bosses promptly instigated huge wage cuts. A national strike was called and the miners sought the help of transport and rail workers without success. The strikers were locked out by the owners and over 600,000 families were forced onto the Poor Law before a new government subsidy prepared the way for a settlement.

By 1922 prices had continued to fall and working people had to grudgingly accept lower wages. With unemployment very high there was a falling off in the number of strikes. It seemed it was only the sheer force of Lloyd George's personality that kept the coalition afloat, but in November another election was called. The Tories were returned under Bonar Law, whilst Labour gained more seats than the Liberals. Lloyd George was brought down in part by his flagrant sale of honours. In 1921 over a hundred new peers and baronets were appointed by donating generously to the prime minister's private political fund. King George let it be known that he was none too impressed by a succession of rich no-hopers being appointed to the Upper House. The corruption of the coalition under Lloyd George enraged the public. Lloyd George duly resigned in the autumn of 1922. In the same year Ellis and Co., one of London's oldest stockbroking firms, failed and its senior partner disappeared. He was arrested months later and jailed for publishing a false balance sheet.

Indecisive elections followed. The votes were increasingly being split three ways. The Liberals won 29.7 per cent of the vote in 1923, a figure they were subsequently never able to match. By October 1924 a third election in two years was called. The campaign was overshadowed by an exposé in the *Daily Mail* stating that a letter sent from the president of Communist International to the British representative of the Comintex Executive was encouraging revolutionary sentiment amongst sympathisers of the Labour Party. Although subsequently thought to have been a forgery, it had the effect of sending Liberal voters scurrying into the Tory camp. The three-party system was seen by the public as bringing instability and in 1924 the reassuring figure of Stanley Baldwin became prime minister with a huge majority.

Trouble in the mines was brewing again. Before the war, Britain had exported huge quantities of coal, but high domestic consumption and a fall in productivity had allowed other producers to fill the shortfall. The matter was made worse by a plan that allowed Germany to export to France at heavily subsidised prices as part of a reparation agreement. Britain's re-entry into the Gold Standard in 1925 also had the effect of making sterling uncompetitive. The mine owners weren't happy (they rarely were!). They announced a reduction in wages and longer working hours. The TUC backed the miners in their dispute. The battle lines were being drawn. Enter Stanley Baldwin with the offer of a nine-month subsidy to help maintain the miners' earnings whilst yet another royal commission pondered the problem. Whilst suggesting a massive reorganisation of the industry, the commission also advised a withdrawal of the subsidy and a huge reduction in pay rates for the miners to maintain the industry's profitability. Not satisfied with this, the owners also demanded a longer working week in their new terms of employment. They also stated that anyone not accepting their terms would be locked out. Even King George appeared sympathetic to the miners. He was quoted as saying, 'Try living on their wages before you judge them.'

His voice went unheard. The blue touch paper had been lit. Over a million miners were locked out. Negotiations with the TUC broke down and a General Strike was called on 3rd May 1926. Crucially on this occasion, rail, transport, steel and print workers came out in support. For nine days all services were paralysed, with the docks at a standstill for a time. The seamen's union, however, rejected the strike call and electricity supplies were maintained.

The government had planned for the eventuality of a prolonged dispute. Working through local commissioners they managed to mobilise volunteers to man London buses and unload vessels at the docks. Students and ex-service personnel drove trams and buses, stoked fire stations and generally gave the appearance of enjoying themselves. The TUC was not. It soon became clear that the public appeared prepared to endure a long strike if necessary. The mood turned against the strikers. There were dire warnings of anarchy taking over. The TUC was alarmed as half its reserves were eaten up by strike pay. Then the picket lines at London's docks were broken by the army and vital goods started to be distributed again.

Worse was to follow. Unions opposed to the strike took the TUC to court. Here Justice Astbury declared the strike to be illegal and the TUC realised it was liable to huge fines. On 12th May the TUC went to Downing Street and informed the prime minister that the strike was being called off. The miners fought on until October when dreadful hardship forced them back to work. The owners refused to re-employ those they deemed to be troublemakers, whilst the rest were forced to accept longer hours and lower wages. The anger and resentment lingered and festered for generations to come and provided a touchstone for ongoing acrimonious employment relations.

None of this bothered the Bright Young Things who gallivanted round London knocking back the latest cocktails and generally being vacuous.

The emerging middle classes appeared more interested in upping sticks and making for the respectability of Suburbia. By 1928 hire purchase accounted for half the sales of cars and furniture for the home. The foul weather reflected the increasingly dire state of the economy. Torrential rain caused the Thames to flood, with fourteen Londoners being drowned. Unemployment continued to haunt the country. The Liberals' Yellow Book proposed a £250 million public works programme to give employment to an extra 600,000. It was easy for them to make grandiose plans for, by now, they had little chance of being elected. Stanley Baldwin, meantime, was promising to lead the country to a new era of prosperity. For all his soothing manner there was plenty of discontent within his own party. The 1929 election saw the Tories lose 150 seats, many to the ailing Liberals, but it was the Labour party that was returned with the most seats, but not enough to gain an overall majority.

In a striking parallel to today's political scene, the Liberal leader Lloyd George complained that with twenty-three per cent of the vote, the party only won nine per cent of the seats, and called for proportional representation.

By 1929 world trade was collapsing, and coupled with the speculative boom in shares in America, it proved to be a toxic mix. Ordinary citizens were borrowing huge sums to invest in the market. It couldn't last. It didn't.

On 24th October 1929 the bubble burst leading to panic selling. The contagion quickly crossed the Atlantic and spread throughout the world. Britain, a leading trading nation, saw its markets collapsing. Unemployment soared to over 2.5 million. Prime Minister Ramsay MacDonald recorded in his diary, 'The whole economic system is breaking down.'

So the decade ended in turmoil. Stories circulated of investors diving off skyscrapers in New York. Certainly in the City people lost fortunes overnight. Most, though, were just corks in the sea, tossed and buffeted by the financial storm raging around them. Ninety years on, little seems to have changed. Greed still flourishes and we repeat the mistakes of our predecessors. However, Londoners generally continue to have the capacity for turning their backs on problems that they can't control. With a couple of drinks inside them, or a trip to the cinema, they can forget those silver-tongued politicians and reckless bankers and get on with the serious business of enjoying themselves and their iconic capital.

Bibliography

Baker, Michael, *London Transport in the 1920s* (Ian Allen Publishing, 2009)

Breeze, Charlotte, *Hutch* (Bloomsbury, 1999)

Craddock, Harry, *The Savoy Cocktail Book* (Pavilion, 1999)

Davis, John, *A History of Britain 1885–1939* (Macmillan Press, 1988)

Glinert, Ed, *The London Compendium* (Penguin Books, 2003)

Glinert, Ed, *West End Chronicles* (Penguin Books, 2008)

Hobhouse, Hermione, *Regent Street* (Phillimore, 2008)

Jackson, Alan, *London's Metroland* (Capital History, 2006)

Jenkins, Alan, *The Twenties* (Peerage Books, 1974)

Laver, James, *Costume and Fashion* (Thames & Hudson, 1995)

Linnane, Fergus, *London's Underworld* (Robson Books, 2003)

Montgomery-Massingberd, Hugh, *The London Ritz* (Aurum Press, 1980)

McConkey, Kenneth, *Sir John Lavery* (Cannongate Press, 1993)

Mitchell, Sally, *The Dictionary of British Equestrian Artists* (Antique Collectors Club, 1985)

Morton, James, *Gangland* (Warner Books, 1993)

Ross, Cathy, *Twenties' London: A City in the Jazz Age* (Philip Wilson, 2003)

Roye, *Nude Ego* (Hutchinson, 1955)

Summers, Judith, *Soho* (Bloomsbury, 1989)

Tames, Richard, *Soho Past* (Historical Publications, 1994)

Taylor, D. J., *Bright Young People* (Vintage Books, 2008)

Towler, Edward (Ed.), *British Dance Bands, 1920–49* (General Gramophone Publications, 1985)

Waugh, Evelyn, and Davie, Michael (Ed.), *The Diaries of Evelyn Waugh* (Penguin Books, 1982)

Wilson, Julian, *The Great Race Horse* (Little Brown, 1987)

Windsor, Alan, *Modern British Painting* (Scolar Press, 1992)

Photo Acknowledgements

The author and publisher are grateful to the following for permission to reproduce the illustrations included in this book:

The Mary Evans Picture Library
The Savoy Hotel
The John Lewis Partnership
Bruce Calvert

Other illustrations supplied by the author.